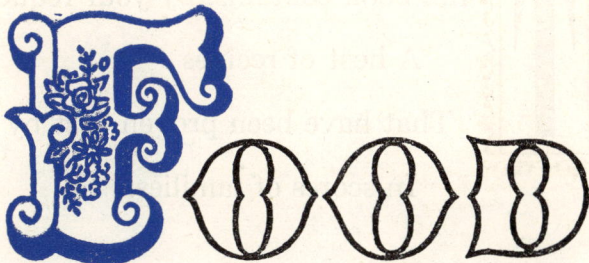

C0-CZU-430

FOOD

FOR THE BODY

FOR THE SOUL

This book contains, by your request,
  A host of recipes
That have been proven best by test
  In scores of families.

And for your soul's delight as well,
  You'll cherish it we know,
For with sweet nectar from above,
  Its pages overflow.

So may it prove a friend indeed,
  As you its contents scan,
Minist'ring to your spirit's need
  And to the "inner-man."

Avis B. Christiansen

FOOD

FOR THE BODY

FOR THE SOUL

MOODY PRESS

153 Institute Place

Chicago, Illinois

Copyright
1943
by
The Moody Bible Institute
of Chicago

1ST PRINTING DEC. 1943
2ND PRINTING JUNE 1944
3RD PRINTING AUG. 1944
4TH PRINTING OCT. 1944
5TH PRINTING JAN. 1945
6TH PRINTING SEPT. 1945
7TH PRINTING JUNE 1946
8TH PRINTING JUNE 1947
Printed in the U. S. A.

Mrs. Frances Youngren
Director of WMBI
Home Hour

Foreword

Home is not just a place where we eat and sleep, but it is the endeared dwelling place where domestic love, happy and cherished family life, rest, peace, and shelter from an evil world are known and enjoyed. Home is the place where we are treated the best, but complain the most. The home was established by God and in His plan for mankind. The family unit is that upon which the whole social structure of humanity and the fabric of civilization rests. If the home goes, the nation goes.

This book is dedicated to the American home. Joshua, just before God called him away from this earthly scene, committed his home and progenity unto the Lord. "But as for me and my house, we will serve the Lord" (Joshua 24:15). What a spiritual awakening there would be in our land today if more of our homes were dedicated to serving the Lord!

We take this opportunity to thank all those who have had part in making this book possible. Wherever possible, we have traced the origin of material used and given due credit. We thank the homemakers who answered our call on the Home Hour for their favorite recipes, as well as those who have helped to contribute "bits of rhyme and prose, and a spiritual message to help you to keep looking up beyond the dishpan and the broom."

Until He comes, "keep your home near Heaven; let it face the Father's house."

Mrs. Frances Youngren

CONTENTS

TOMATO JUICE COCKTAIL

1 No. 3 can tomato juice
1 small onion thinly sliced
1 teaspoon granulated sugar
½ teaspoon salt
1 teaspoon minced parsley
1 bay leaf
1 stalk celery bruised

Combine and chill 15 minutes or longer, strain.

Mrs. Earl Sanders

TOMATO COCKTAIL

½   bushel tomatoes
4   green sweet peppers
1   bunch celery
1½ cups sugar
4   medium dry onions
½   bunch parsley
12   whole cloves
½   cup salt

Boil all together, gently at first, until all juices flow. Then simmer ½ hour. Strain and re-heat. Pour into sterilized jars and seal. The juice of 2 lemons and 1 teaspoon Worcestershire sauce may be added after straining, before re-heating. Usually add the juice of 1 lemon to 1 quart of cocktail just before serving.

Miss Talka H. Wubbena

CALIFORNIA FRUIT HORS d'OEUVRES

All these hors d'oeuvres may be arranged on individual serving plates or on one large platter.

Fill large cooked, pitted prunes with cream cheese mixed with a little cream, chopped nuts, salt and paprika to taste.

Dip pineapple segments in finely chopped pecan meats.

Marinate ½-inch slices of banana in slightly sweetened lemon juice. When ready to serve, drain thoroughly, place on serving dish. Decorate with whipped cream or cream cheese which has been thinned with cream.

Dip skinned orange sections into fruit juice and roll in toasted cocoanut.

Marinate whole figs in orange juice. Dip in grated lemon rind and garnish with slivers of blanched almonds.

SHRIMP COCKTAIL SAUCE

½ cup chili sauce
⅓ cup celery (finely chopped)
8 drops Tabasco sauce
1 tablespoon lemon juice
1 tablespoon Worcestershire sauce
2 teaspoons horseradish
Lemon

Combine ingredients and serve with the shrimp in cocktail cups, using a wedge of lemon for garnish. Or, arrange the shrimp on lettuce leaves, on individual serving plates, using the cocktail sauce for topping.

FEASTING ON THE WORD

Thy words were found, and I did eat them. (Jer. 15:16)

We will note from this verse that God does not want us to merely *taste* His Word, but to *eat* it—make it a part of ourselves.

There are several things that make up a good meal, and thank God, Jesus is able to supply every one of them.

The Psalmist said: "Thou preparest a table before me in the presence of mine enemies" (Psalm 23:5).

We have a most wonderful guest to eat with us. Jesus said, "I will come in to him, and will sup with him" (Rev. 3:20).

Linen is provided; "The fine linen is the righteous acts of the saints" (Rev. 19:8, R. V.).

Our God has a cup provided—"My cup runneth over" (Psalm 23:5).

Our knife? Turn to Hebrews 4:12. Thy "word is sharper than any two-edged sword."

Our table is now ready for the food. What shall our food be?

"I have treasured up the words of his mouth more than my necessary food" (Job 23:12, R. V.).

On the menu today we have the following:

MEAT—"My meat is to do the will of him that sent me" (John 4:34).

SALT—"Let your speech be .... seasoned with salt" (Col. 4:6).

BREAD—"Man doth not live by bread only, but by every word that proceedeth out of the mouth of the Lord doth man live" (Deut. 8:3).

BUTTER—"Butter and honey shall he eat" (Isa. 7:15).

HONEY—".... and it was in my mouth as honey for sweetness" (Ezek. 3:3). (See also the text.)

MILK—"I fed you with milk" (I Cor. 3:2, R. V.).

FRUIT—"The fruit of the Spirit is love, joy, peace, longsuffering, gentleness, goodness, faith, meekness, temperance" (Gal. 5:22, 23).

Thus we have a good meal for the child of God. After partaking of such a meal, the child of God is provided with certain vitamins:

Vitamin A—Ambition
Vitamin B—Brightness
Vitamin C—Confidence
Vitamin D—Determination
Vitamin E—Enthusiasm

Thus, God's child can go out and win the battle against Satan and sin. This can be done, for "Thy words were found, and I did eat them."

NOTE: This sermon makes a good object lesson for children. Use the articles mentioned: table, linen, bread, etc., for illustration.

Rev. C. P. Smales, Placerville, Calif.
The Biblical Digest

BACON AND TOMATO CANAPE

Toast rounds of bread the size of tomato slices. Spread with mixture of crisp, chopped bacon blended with mayonnaise. Over this place a slice of tomato, then a slice of cucumber. Top with a slice of stuffed olive.

Mrs. Gust Carlson

CRANBERRY COCKTAIL

2 cups cranberries
¼ cup orange juice
2 cups water
¼ cup lemon juice
Sugar to taste

Cook berries in water until soft. Let drip through a jelly bag. Bring to boil. Add juices. Sweeten to taste. Stir until sugar is dissolved. Chill.

Mrs. Earl Sanders

"APPLE RINGS"

2 red apples, washed and polished

1 cup sugar

1 cup water

3 tablespoons red cinnamon candy

Do not pare the apples. Remove the cores and slice each apple crosswise in ¾ inch thick slices. Bring the sugar and the water to a boil, and stir until sugar dissolves. Boil 4 minutes with the red cinnamon candy in the syrup. Drop the apple rings into syrup. Cover and simmer gently until fruit is tender. Garnish meat platter with them. This is palatable as well as decorative.

Mrs. Doris Landers

APPLESAUCE LENDS ITSELF TO VARIATIONS

Try some of these tempting applesauce variations when meals need a pickup:

1. Spread applesauce on crisp waffles, pancakes, or French toast.

2. Flavor with mint and tint a delicate green color. Serve with all types of lamb dishes.

3. Flavor with cinnamon and tint pink. Serve with pork.

4. Combine with cream cheese and ground peanuts and use as a sandwich spread with lettuce. Add finely chopped celery if desired.

5. Add 1 tablespoon lemon juice and 2 tablespoons prepared horseradish to 2 cups applesauce for a delicious relish.

6. Spread thick, strained applesauce between graham crackers, stacked 4 or 5 high; frost with lemon icing or serve with soft custard topping.

7. Delmonico apples: put a layer of applesauce in a buttered baking dish, sprinkle with ground almonds or peanuts, dot with butter, and sprinkle with crushed macaroons. Add a small amount of water and bake for 15 minutes in moderately hot oven (400° F.).

8. Beat two egg whites until light and beat in 4 tablespoons sugar and ½ teaspoon baking powder. Beat until stiff but not dry. Fold in 1 cup thick strained applesauce. Spread applesauce meringue on squares of leftover cake, and brown lightly in oven or broiler.

9. Add ¼ pound of cooked dried apricots or an equal amount of fresh apricot pulp to 2 cups applesauce. The flavor is unusually good.

10. Place a deep layer of applesauce in buttered baking dish, cover with marshmallows, cut into eighths, and add another layer of applesauce. Top with marshmallow halves and place in a hot oven until marshmallows are puffed.

11. Cook apples with bananas and a small stick of cinnamon until apples are tender. Force through a sieve, sweeten with sugar, and serve hot or cold.

12. Serve applesauce on hot gingerbread instead of whipped cream.

Mary Meade—Chicago Tribune

CLEAN HANDS

Once, in my childhood days long gone and dead,
I watched a supper table being spread
By busy hands; and eagerly I said—
Wishing to help—"Please, may I bring the bread?"
Gently, reprovingly, a kind voice said,
"Are your hands clean?"

Oft, when I see the multitude, unfed,
And waiting hungry for the living bread,
My heart and hands are eager to be sped
To bring the manna that they may be fed.
But One Voice says, e'en as a voice once said,
"Are your hands clean?"
                      I only bow my head.

Mrs. Eddie Dunshie

❧

I said to a man that stood at the gate of the year: "Give me a
light that I might go safely into the unknown." And he said to me—
"Go out into the darkness and put your hand into the hand of God.
That shall be better to thee than a light and safer than a known
way."

❧

He came to my desk with quivering lip—
    The lesson was done—
"Dear Teacher, I want a new leaf," he said,
    "I have spoiled this one."
In place of the leaf so stained and blotted,
I gave him a new one all unspotted,
    And into his sad eyes smiled,
    "Do better now, my child."

I went to the Throne with a quivering soul
    The old year was done—
"Dear Father, hast Thou a new leaf for me?
    I have spoiled this one."
He took the old leaf, stained and blotted,
And gave me a new one all unspotted,
    And into my sad heart smiled,
    "Do better now, my child."

Author unknown

NORWEGIAN FRUKT SUPPE (Fruit Soup)

½ cup pearl tapioca
3 cups water
½ cup cooked raisins
½ cup cooked pitted prunes
Juice of 1 lemon
Sugar to taste

Cook tapioca in water until transparent. Then add raisins, prunes, lemon juice and sugar. Simmer over low fire for 3 or 4 minutes; serve hot or cold.

BORSCHT (A Famous Russian Soup)

1 bunch beets
1 cup tomatoes, fresh or canned
4 cups water
1 small onion
½ pound breast of beef
1 tablespoon lemon juice
¼ cup sugar
¼ teaspoon salt
4 eggs

Pare beets and cut them into long strips. Strain tomatoes over beets, not letting any seeds through. Add water. Put in the onion and meat, cut into small pieces, and simmer for 30 minutes. Add lemon juice, sugar and salt. Boil one-half hour more. Beat the eggs with pinch of salt. Add the hot borscht to this, a little at a time, stirring well to prevent the separating of the eggs. This will be more or less like a soft custard mixture. Serve at once, while hot.

WINTRY DAY SOUP

1½ pounds ground gooseneck meat
1 teaspoon salt
½ teaspoon allspice
1 bunch celery
1 bunch carrots
1 large onion
2 or 3 parsnips
Potatoes (optional)

Roll seasoned meat in small balls about 1¼ inches in diameter and drop as you roll them into kettle containing 3 quarts cold water and 1 tablespoon salt. Place over medium low burner. Water will gradually become hotter so meat juice does not escape from last of meat balls. Skim the soup. Add 1 bunch celery, 1 bunch carrots, 1 large onion, 2 or 3 parsnips which have been cut up. Also potatoes if desired. Simmer at least one hour. 10 large servings.

DUMPLINGS

2 cups flour
4 teaspoons baking powder
½ teaspoon salt
½ cup milk
2 beaten eggs

Mix and sift the flour, baking powder and salt. Add the milk and beaten eggs. Drop quickly by spoonfuls into soup, cover closely and steam 12 minutes.

I AM RESOLVED . . .

As a Mother

1. To make this coming year count in the development of my own spiritual life and that of my family, even though I realize there will be plenty to hinder me. "My sufficiency is of Him."

> *Comment.* New Year's resolutions are short-lived as a rule, but any mother who determines within herself to feed daily on the "hidden manna" is bound to show marked deepening of her inner life.

2. To take this task seriously, to give time to planning for it and carrying it out, also to checking up on myself so that one day may build on another.

> *Comment.* Without doing this, mother, it is useless to begin. To take time every day to analyze one's actions and thoughts, even though done hurriedly occasionally, is the way to success.

3. To read my Bible once a day at least, twice or three times if possible until I get a message for myself. In some cases this may mean only one verse; in others, many more. But I am determined to read thoughtfully.

> *Comment.* By doing this you will find your other resolutions simplified. The key that unlocks the door to "a closer walk with God" is Bible reading and prayer.

4. To spend more time in prayer, expecting results therefrom. My prayer life must be inspirational and edifying, not mere routine.

> *Comment.* The average Christian does not draw on his prayer resources. The one who has learned to obey the command "Pray without ceasing" (a calling on God to meet every need), has a powerful weapon always at hand.

5. To cultivate the habit of "giving thanks in all things" and of "praising Him at all times." I began doing this last year and found there was no time for grouches, self-pity and fear.

> *Comment.* A wonderful secret for any Christian to learn. That little word "all" leaves no room for Satan to take advantage. Those who have tried it know it works.

6. To be more careful to maintain a Christian atmosphere in the home. This means I must watch the literature that comes in, the radio programs, table conversations, conduct one toward another, unkindly comments and gossip.

> *Comment.* This seems to be peculiarly the mother's job. Yet family co-operation is essential in carrying it out.

7. Not to become discouraged if I do not attain these resolutions all at once. They are all good and should be carried out. With God's help (and I can be sure of that) I should be in good running

ONION SOUP (French Recipe)

4 large Bermuda onions
2 tablespoons butter
2 tablespoons flour
6 bouillon cubes
6 slices toasted bread
6 tablespoons grated cheese
6 cups water
Seasoning to taste

Chop onions finely, brown in butter over slow fire. Mix with flour, stirring well. Season with salt and pepper (a pinch of thyme gives it zest). Pour in 6 cups bouillon already prepared and let simmer half hour. Pour soup into individual crocks and put one slice of toast on top. Cover toast with grated cheese and then put crocks in broiler to brown. Serve soup in wide soup plates or in the individual crocks.

DUTCH SPLIT PEA SOUP

1 pound split green peas

1 medium sized carrot

3 onions

3 potatoes

1 heaping teaspoon salt

Pepper

½ pound metwurst sausage

The metwurst sausage may be bought at any butcher who caters to Holland trade. Or it may be substituted with a meaty soup or ham bone. Into a cooking kettle place all the above ingredients (the vegetables are diced). Add about 3 quarts cold water. Bring to a boil and boil gently for about 2 hours, stirring occasionally. Add a little more water while it is cooking, if necessary. Serve very hot with crisp crackers. This soup has been served in our family for 3 generations and is a special favorite.

Mrs. Samuel Ekema

RUSSIAN BEET SOUP

2 quarts boiling water
8 beef bouillon cubes or 2 quarts strong stock
3 onions (medium size)
1 tablespoon sugar
2 cups chopped cabbage
1 bay leaf
1 teaspoon pepper
1 teaspoon salt
¼ cup flour
½ cup water
1 ½ cups cooked beets
½ cup soured cream

Cook the first eight ingredients slowly for 10 minutes. Make a paste of the flour and water. Stir into the bouillon mixture. Add beets which have been chopped. Heat to boiling point, stirring constantly. Remove from heat and stir in ½ cup thick soured cream. Serve at once. Serves six.

CREAM OF ASPARAGUS SOUP

2 No. 1 tins asparagus, or 2 medium bunches fresh asparagus, cooked
2 ¾ cups fresh pasteurized milk
¼ cup whipping cream
2 tablespoons butter
2 tablespoons flour
1 tablespoon chopped parsley
1 slice onion
1 ½ teaspoons salt
½ teaspoon sugar

Remove 10 choice tips of asparagus to be used for garnish. Chop rest of asparagus fine, or press through a puree sieve; there should be at least 2 cups puree and liquid. Put milk and cream in double boiler, add onion and heat to scalding point. Remove onion. Melt butter, blend in flour, and add salt and sugar. Add scalded milk and cream slowly, stirring vigorously and cook over hot water, for 15 minutes. Add asparagus puree and parsley. Heat thoroughly, add tips and serve at once. 2 chicken bouillon cubes added to milk produce a delicious variation in flavor.

Yield: 5 servings.

14

order before many months pass, which means that our home life will be more pleasing to our Lord whose approval we covet.

    Comment. These seven simple determinations on the part of any mother of a family faithfully acted upon will bring heaven much closer to this earth and set the "joy-bells" ringing above.

As a Father

1. To back up Mother in her splendid plans for the family, do my share, and not make excuses and alibis.

    Comment. If more fathers would do this, it would not only lighten the task for the mother, but have a decided influence on the children, both present and future.

2. To take time for my own personal Bible reading and prayer, even though some other things have to be left undone.

    Comment. Even the family devotions cannot give a father the spiritual tone that a few minutes alone with God can do. Time spent this way pays great dividends.

3. To attend church and Sunday School regularly and quit making excuses which are getting to be a habit. This is one good example I can set the children.

    Comment. And a more far-reaching one than most fathers realize. It affects generations to come.

4. To give up personal desires when the children's good is at stake.

    Comment. This takes wisdom and good judgment, for after all, a father has some rights that must not be overridden.

5. To play and sing with the children on occasions and to know their friends.

    Comment. This makes for real fellowship which breeds confidence and gives a father influence.

6. To guide the children in their choice of reading matter and radio programs.

    Comment. A worthy resolve but not easily carried out for lack of time. It will need both parents to cope with these problems.

7. To make our family more cooperative.

    Comment. This is the solution to many problems. To talk things over in a friendly way and co-ordinate the daily lessons with daily living is the way to develop strong and enduring family life.

Esther W. Turner
Church School Promoter

FISH

BAKED STUFFED FISH

Oily varieties of fish are best for baking because they cook in their own fat and require no basting, and the skin will keep its shape without cracking. Lean or dry meated fish should be brushed with melted fat before baking, or strips of bacon may be laid over the top. Lean varieties also need to be basted frequently during baking. Fish may be baked with or without the head and tail. Sprinkle the cleaned fish with salt inside and out. Stuff the fish loosely, leaving room for the dressing to expand. Fasten with toothpicks, and lace with string or use metal skewers, or needle and thread.

When baking a large fish, lay a piece of oiled cheesecloth in the bottom of the baking pan. This will make it possible to lift the fish from the pan without breaking after baking. If desired, several strips of bacon may be arranged in the baking pan, and the fish placed on them for baking. Bake in a hot oven (425° F.) and allow 10 minutes per pound baking time for fish weighing up to 4 pounds, and 5 minutes for each additional pound. When tender, remove carefully from the pan, take out fasteners used to secure the dressing in the fish, and serve whole on a hot platter.

STUFFED BAKED PIKE

Fish

3 medium sized tomatoes

1 cup raw, finely cubed potatoes

¼ cup chopped green peppers

1 tablespoon butter

¾ teaspoon salt

⅛ teaspoon black pepper

Split the fish lengthwise to clean it, being careful not to tear skin, then dry. Dice the tomatoes, mix with the cubed potatoes. Add the green pepper, salt and pepper. Place the stuffing in the fish, sew the opening with stout thread. Put fish on greased rack in baking pan. Rub outside of fish with salt and brush with fat, or place several strips of bacon over top. Bake in moderately slow oven (325° F.) for 1 hour and a half.

Mrs. Effie Willemin

BAKED SPANISH MACKEREL

Fish (Whitefish, or Striped Bass may be used)

DRESSING:

1 cup coarsely broken soda crackers

½ of 8-ounce can of drained button mushrooms

¼ cup minced parsley

1 small onion, finely chopped

Clean fish, remove bone, rub the inside and out with salt, fill fish with mushroom dressing. Toss together the crackers, mushrooms, parsley, and onion and moisten all with mushroom liquor. Then fasten edges of fish together with wooden skewers, or sew with strong thread. Brush stuffed fish with melted fat and arrange on a greased rack on well-oiled brown wrapping paper. Bake uncovered in a moderately hot oven 375° to 400° F. Allow 10 minutes to the pound for a fish under 4 pounds. When done, remove skewers, serve on a hot platter with sauteed mushrooms (other ½ of the can). Brown the mushrooms in 2 tablespoons butter, arrange these around the fish on platter, garnishing with sliced tomatoes and radish roses.

Mrs. Doris Landers

SHRIMP COCKTAIL SAUCE, See Page 8

Courtesy Booth Fisheries Corp.

Courtesy Booth Fisheries Corp.

BAKED STUFFED FISH, See Page 16 ➡

CREAM OF ASPARAGUS, See Page 14

Courtesy Bowman Dairy Co.

Courtesy Bowman Dairy Co.

BORSCHT, See Page 12

LIFE-GIVING VITAMINS

In the last few years we have been consistently educated in the knowledge and use of vitamins. They are the regulators of food substances, and are recognized as indispensable to normal growth, disease prevention and the maintenance of general health:

Our health authorities tell us that vitamins are classified into types. Each performs some specific function. Beauty demands close acquaintance and daily use of all these vitamins.

Vitamin A

Vitamin A, or Acceptance Vitamin, stands for new life or life eternal. It is when we realize, as did the prophet Isaiah that we are unclean that we are ready to do something about it. You remember how Isaiah cried out, "Woe is me! for I am undone; because I am a man of unclean lips, and I dwell in the midst of a people of unclean lips" (Isa. 6:5). We must realize that "the heart is deceitful above all things, and desperately wicked" (Jer. 17:9). It is then we really need help, for we ourselves are powerless to help. We naturally wonder where to turn or what to do. And then, we hear the Great Physician inviting us to come to Him. He says, "Him that cometh to me I will in no wise cast out" (John 6:37). "I will cast away from you all your transgressions . . . . and make you a new heart and a new spirit" (Ezek. 18:31).

You see, "Christ died for our sins" (1 Cor. 15:3), and it is only by accepting Him as our Saviour that we have this new, eternal life, which is His gift to us. We can never find spiritual health and happiness without the use of the Acceptance Vitamin.

Vitamin B

Vitamin B, or the Belief Vitamin, is essential to the development and normal functioning of the new life. Our Great Physician explains that "all things are possible to him that believeth" (Mark 9:23). "Believe on the Lord Jesus Christ, and thou shalt be saved" (Acts 16:31).

The joyous exuberance of youth and the hearty vigor of old age owe their existence to Vitamin A, Acceptance Vitamin and their continued well-being to the Belief Vitamin.

TUNA AND NOODLE AU GRATIN

3 tablespoons butter
2 tablespoons flour
1 ½ cups milk
1 teaspoon salt
¼ teaspoon pepper
½ teaspoon paprika
½ pound American cheese, grated
1 small can mushrooms
17 ½ ounce can Tuna fish
14 ounce package noodles

Make white sauce of butter, milk, flour and seasonings. Add cheese and stir until smooth. Place mushrooms, flaked tuna and noodles in greased baking dish in order named with cheese sauce between each layer. Garnish with a few mushrooms. Bake in 400° F. oven for 20 minutes, or until golden brown. Serves 6. Cheese may be omitted if desired.

Miss Cleda Smith

SALMON-LIMA BEAN CASSEROLE

1 11-ounce can salmon
1 11-ounce can lima beans (or equal amount cooked fresh or dry beans)
1 cup medium white sauce
½ cup fine dry bread crumbs, buttered

Arrange flaked salmon and lima beans in alternate rows in greased casserole, over which pour white sauce, and top with buttered crumbs. Cover, and bake in medium hot oven (350° F.) for half an hour, remove cover, and brown crumbs.

Mrs. Robert D. Wyatt

CREAMED CRABMEAT IN SHELLS (6 Servings)

½ cup diced celery
¼ cup diced green pepper
3 tablespoons butter
1 cup milk
3 tablespoons flour
½ teaspoon salt
Black pepper
1 ¼ cups flaked crabmeat (6 ½-ounce can)

Cook celery in a very small amount of water for 15 minutes. Add green pepper after 10 minutes. Melt butter in a sauce pan, blend in flour and add milk. Stir constantly over direct heat until sauce thickens. Now add cooked celery and green pepper, also salt. Combine with crabmeat, from which all bits of cartilage have been removed. Pour mixture into buttered baking shells (or individual casseroles), sprinkle with buttered crumbs and brown in hot oven (425° F.) for about 15 minutes. Chilled cranberry sauce is excellent served with this.

Mrs. Doris Landers

OYSTERS A LA KING

1 pint oysters
2 cups milk and oyster liquid
3 tablespoons butter
3 tablespoons flour
1 small can mushrooms, drained
¼ cup chopped green pepper
2 tablespoons minced pimiento
1 ½ teaspoons salt
⅛ teaspoon pepper
Buttered toast

Simmer oysters in their own liquid for 5 minutes. Drain thoroughly, saving the liquid and adding enough milk to make 2 cups liquid. Saute mushrooms in butter for 5 minutes. Stir in flour and make a medium sauce with liquid. Then add remaining ingredients, except oysters and toast. Simmer until thick. Add oysters. Serve on toast. This will serve four.

Mrs. Gertrude Hansen

18

Vitamin C

Vitamin C, Confession Vitamin, must be used daily to keep one in perfect condition. "If we confess our sins, he is faithful and just to forgive us our sins, and cleanse us from all unrighteousness" (I John 1:9).

Vitamin D

Now we come to that very necessary Vitamin D, Determination Vitamin. This has a wonderful effect on one's backbone, which, of course, is vital to good posture. A wobbly backbone ruins posture, but, with Vitamin D daily on the job, one has no fear. Simply determine "not to know any thing . . . . save Jesus Christ, and him crucified" (I Cor. 2:2).

Vitamin E

Vitamin E, the well-known and absolutely necessary Endurance Vitamin, is a demanded element of true beauty. "Therefore endure hardness, as a good soldier of Jesus Christ" (II Tim. 2:3), remembering that "he that shall endure unto the end, the same shall be saved" (Matt. 24:13).

Don't fail to use daily these vitamins so necessary to beauty and health.

Mrs. Estelle M. Grant
Christian Beacon

THREE GATES

If you are tempted to reveal
A tale someone to you has told
About another, make it pass
Before you speak, three gates of gold,
Three narrow gates: First, "Is it true?"
Then "Is it needful?" In your mind
Give truthful answer, and the next
Is last and narrowest, "Is it kind?"
And if to reach your lips at last
It passes through these gateways three,
Then you may tell, nor ever fear
What the result of speech may be.

True Living

SHEPHERD'S PIE

3 pounds lean beef, chuck or flank
Suet
1 clove garlic
1 quart boiling water
1 bay leaf
1 tablespoon salt
½ teaspoon pepper
3 tablespoons catsup
1 teaspoon Worcestershire sauce
1 teaspoon sugar
Few sprigs parsley
4 medium onions
½ cup celery (optional)
6 carrots
1 yellow turnip
Kitchen Bouquet
Flour
Mashed potatoes

Cut the beef into 1½-inch cubes. Heat the kettle in which you're going to cook the meat and vegetables—and incidentally, a Dutch Oven is excellent. When kettle is hot, drop in some suet cut up in 1-inch cubes, and the clove garlic. When suet sputters and garlic is beginning to brown a little, put meat in the hot kettle to brown, turning it with a fork. When meat is nice and brown, add the boiling water, bay leaf, salt, pepper, catsup, Worcestershire sauce, sugar, parsley, onions and celery. Cover the kettle and let simmer at least 1½ hours, usually a little longer. Then add the carrots and yellow turnip and let simmer another hour or until everything is meltingly tender. Thicken with flour and water and a little Kitchen Bouquet, that adds flavor to the gravy. Place this in a large casserole or baking dish, cover with mashed white potatoes which, of course, have been boiled separately and mashed with plenty of butter or margarine. Cover the meat and vegetables with the mashed potatoes, and to make it a bit fancy punch holes with the bowl of a teaspoon in the potatoes and fill the holes with catsup. Put into the oven to brown, and you have a delicious, good-looking one course meal.

Mrs. T. G. Lindsay

NEW ENGLAND BOILED DINNER

4 pounds brisket of corned beef
3 quarts water
4 medium-sized potatoes
8 small onions
8 small carrots
1 medium-sized head of cabbage

Allow about 4 hours for cooking the beef. Cook over low heat. Add prepared vegetables (cabbage cut in quarters) and cook about 30 minutes. Drain meat and vegetables and serve at once.

Mrs. Wm. G. Hamstra

TALERINE ONE DISH MEAL

Minced onion
½ pound ground beef
1 can condensed tomato soup
1 can water
1 can corn niblets, or ½ larger
can cream style corn
1½ cups noodles, cooked
6 to 10 stuffed olives

Put the mixed ingredients in a buttered casserole and bake in oven at 350° F. for 20 to 30 minutes. Talerine makes a delicious and satisfying meal for 3 or 4.

Mrs. Claude Neubauer

REMEMBRANCE

I thank my God upon every remembrance of you.

(Philippians 1:3)

I want you to know you are never forgotten;
 That the old, old days hid in memory sweet
Are still a part of my life that I cherish—
 Without them so much would be incomplete.
And you are mixed up with so much I remember,
 Your name so often I utter in prayer;
Never forgotten, on earth or in heaven,
 Always the child of God's tenderest care.

I want you to know you are never forgotten,
 That my thoughts and my prayers are folding you round.
Rest in His promises, go where He sends you,
 Do what He bids you, faithful be found.
Look up and trust Him, a new year is dawning,
 Stretch out your hand and take His today;
Bought by Him, loved by Him, never forgotten,
 Hid in His heart forever and aye.

❧

When God measures men He puts the tape around the heart, not the head.

❧

MY ALBUM

My album is a savage breast
Where tempests brood
And shadows rest
 Without one ray of light.

To place the name of Jesus there,
And see that savage kneel in prayer
And point to realms more bright and fair
 —This is my soul's delight.

Robert Moffat

VICTORY MEAT MUFFINS

1 ½ pounds ground beef
3 tablespoons finely chopped onion
¼ cup horseradish
2 eggs
¾ cup cracker crumbs
1 teaspoon salt
⅛ teaspoon black pepper
¼ cup tomato catsup

Line the greased muffin pans with onion rings, pimientos cut as stars, or other designs. Pack the mixture in the pans, leaving about ½ inch space on top of each muffin so the drippings will not run over the pan as muffins cook. Bake in 350° F. oven for 45 minutes. Have a platter of Julienne potatoes ready, place muffins around edge of platter (potatoes in center) and serve immediately. A relish tray of radish roses, celery curls and sweet pickles is a good accompaniment. A beverage and light dessert is a finishing touch for this dinner.

Mrs. Doris Landers

BUDGET STEW

2 tablespoons fat
¾ cup onions sliced
3 cups potatoes diced
1 pound ground beef
¼ cup uncooked rice
1 cup celery diced
2 cups kidney beans (optional)
1 teaspoon salt
⅛ teaspoon pepper
¼ teaspoon chili powder
¼ teaspoon Worcestershire sauce
1 ½ cups tomato juice, or soup

Melt fat in skillet using high heat. Arrange a layer of onions in bottom of pan, next a layer of beef, then rice, and last a layer of potatoes, celery and beans, if used. Combine seasoning and tomato sauce and pour over stew layers. Cover skillet and leave on high heat until steaming freely, then turn heat low and cook 2 to 3 hours. Serves 6 to 8. A green salad and a simple dessert will complete the meal.

Mrs. Seymour C. Clarke

SPAGHETTI ORIENTAL

¼ pound spaghetti (one cup uncooked)
1 pound ground beef
½ pound ground pork
1 medium onion, chopped
1 cup celery
1 can bean sprouts
1 cup tomato soup
½ cup water

Break spaghetti in 2-inch pieces. Cook until tender, about 15 minutes, in 1 quart boiling water to which 1 teaspoon salt has been added. Drain. Brown meat in two tablespoons butter. Then add onion and celery. Simmer slowly 20 minutes in a little water. Mix meat, onion, celery, beans and cooked spaghetti together. Add tomato soup, water and salt. Bake slowly in oven for 1 hour at 350° F.

Mrs. D. N. Benton

WORSTA BROOTJIS (Pigs in Blankets) Holland Recipe

½ pound ground beef
½ pound ground veal
1 egg
½ cup milk
1 rusk
BISCUIT DOUGH:
1 ½ cups flour
1 teaspoon baking powder
½ teaspoon salt
Milk to make soft dough
1 teaspoon meat preparation

Season and mix well the ground meat, egg, milk and rusk. Make a biscuit dough of the other ingredients. Roll dough in thin strips about 4 inches long. Put in large teaspoon of meat preparation. Roll dough securely around meat and close ends well. Bake in 350° F. oven about 30 minutes. Makes 1 dozen.

Mrs. H. Nauta

MEAT DISHES

PRACTICAL WAYS TO EXTEND THIS FINE PROTEIN FOOD OVER MORE MEALS PER WEEK

Meat with cereals 	Meat loaf made with bread crumbs or oatmeal . . . Braised meat with noodles . . . Meat pie . . . Stuffed meats . . . Stew with dumplings . . . Curry with rice . . . Meat balls or sauce or cooked sausage meat with spaghetti or macaroni.
Meat with vegetables 	Stew or pot roast with vegetables . . . Ground meat baked in vegetables . . . Ham shanks with beans . . . Tongue and spinach . . . Braised oxtails or short ribs with vegetables . . . Baked lima beans and bacon squares . . . Shepherd's pie (mashed potato topping).
Meat with eggs 	Diced or ground meat in omelets . . . Soufflés . . . or cooked sausage meat scrambled with eggs.
Meat with milk or cheese 	Creamed meat . . . Salt pork or bacon squares with cream gravy . . . Ham and cheese sandwich . . . Bacon or ham with toasted cheese.
Meat in soup 	Beef barley soup made from soup bone . . . Oxtail soup, with vegetables and rice . . . Split pea soup with ham bone.

Making the most

Serving Meat

Keep the carving knife sharp and cut slices thinner. Use every bit of left-over meat. Vary seasonings for new flavor. Serve meat in different ways — a stew one day, patties or a meat loaf another. Serve good meat gravy more often.

Fewer second helpings. Teach children it's wasteful to leave meat on the plate.

Storing Meat

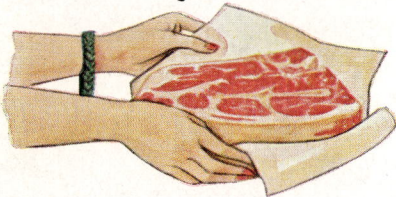

Unwrap fresh meat, cover loosely with waxed paper, store in coldest part of refrigerator. Temperature of 40° to 45° is needed. Use special care with ground meats which spoil more easily than meat in one piece. Cut cooked meat from bone, in large pieces; store, covered, in refrigerator.

MEAT

Buying Meat

There are more different cuts of meat than you realize, perhaps—actually more than 200, including various types of sausage—(yet the average woman knows only 12). Your meat-man has some of them most of the time. All of them are equally nutritious. Try them and see how tasty they really are.

Tricks with Meat

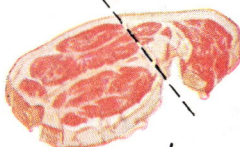

Before you cook the steak, cut off the "tail" and use, ground, next day.

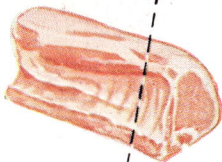

When you buy a loin roast of pork, have a few chops cut off to serve at another meal.

Save meat bones, with a few bits of meat clinging, to use as a soup stock with vegetables.

SAVORY MEAT STEW, made with beef, lamb or veal. Or try a meat loaf or a pot roast with vegetables.

Preparing Meat

Meats shrink less cooked at low temperatures. More good meat juices and better flavor, too.

Learn the right way to cook each cut. Roast or broil tender cuts; braise or simmer cuts that take long, slow cooking. Cook pork thoroughly. Stretch meat flavor by combining it with other foods. Watch for new recipes for liver, sweetbreads and other Variety Meats—for sausage, oxtails and pork feet.

EXTENDING MEAT

MEAT-EXTENDER LOAF
(with mashed potato covering)
(Serves a family of 4 two meals)

1 lb. veal, ground ⎫
½ lb. pork, ground ⎬ or 2¼ lbs. veal, ground.
¾ lb. beef, ground ⎭

½ teaspoon powdered sage
1½ teaspoons salt
½ teaspoon pepper
¼ cup chopped onion
½ cup soft bread crumbs or oatmeal
2 eggs, slightly beaten

⅛ cup liquid (milk or tomato juice)
1 cup peas
1 cup thinly sliced carrots
2½ cups mashed potatoes (quite dry)
¾ cup catchup
Flour

Meat Inserts Courtesy American Meat Institute

Combine all ingredients except potatoes, catchup and flour (reserve 1 tablespoon of beaten egg for brushing potato frosting) and mix well. Pack in medium-sized baking pan. Bake in moderate oven for 1½ hours. Make sauce by thickening liquid from loaf (or use meat drippings or bacon fat) with 2 tablespoons flour blended with cold water for every cup of liquid. Stir in catchup. Unmold meat loaf on baking sheet, frost with mashed potatoes, brush with beaten egg and brown in very hot oven (450° F.).

MY PRAYER

What greeting shall I send you
As I think of you today?
For the wish that I would wish you
Goes beyond what I can say;
Yet unspoken thoughts rise heavenward
In the silence, when we pray.

I will breathe my intercessions
Before God's Altar Throne,
And the best wish I can wish you
Shall be told to Him alone,
And the best thought I can send you
Is from Him, and not my own.

And your name shall be remembered
In the Blessed Presence there
Where remembrances are sacred
And each memory holds a prayer,
And where loving thoughts shall leave you
In a loving Father's care.

Author unknown

ॐ

THINGS I WISH I HAD KNOWN BEFORE I WAS TWENTY-ONE

That my health after thirty depended in a large degree on what
I put into my stomach before I was twenty-one.

How to take care of money.

That a man's habits are mighty hard to change after he is
twenty-one.

That a harvest depends upon the seeds sown.

That things worth while require time, patience, and work.

That you cannot get something for nothing.

The value of absolute truthfulness in everything.

The folly of not taking older people's advice.

That what my mother wanted me to do was right.

That "Dad" wasn't an old fogy after all.

More of the helpful and inspiring messages of the Bible.

The greatness of the opportunity and joy of serving a fellowman.

That Jesus Christ wants to be my Saviour and Friend.

Moody Monthly

SPANISH SPAGHETTI WITH SIZZLED BEEF

⅓ cup finely chopped onion
⅓ cup finely chopped green pepper
3 tablespoons butter or other fat
¾ cup shredded dried beef
1 can cooked spaghetti in tomato sauce (24-ounce)

Cook green pepper and onion in fat until tender. Add beef and brown slightly. Add spaghetti and cook just until thoroughly heated. Seasonings to taste may be added. Serve very hot. Serves 4. Fruit and vegetable salad and a lemon pie will complete the meal.

MEAT BALLS

1 pound hamburger
2 eggs
4 cups corn flakes
1½ cups milk
3 tablespoons chopped onion
1 teaspoon salt
Pepper

Mix well and fry into balls; brown, cover and simmer until well done. Can also be smothered with canned tomatoes after being browned. When I use with tomatoes, I like to cook a head of cabbage in this too, cut in quarters or eighths.
L. Bourne

OUR STANDBY

1 pound chopped beef
¾ cup soda cracker crumbs
1 egg
1 medium onion
¼ cup milk, or less
¾ teaspoon salt
1 tablespoon fat
1 quart of home-made tomato soup, or 1 pint of very rich, or a can of any prepared tomato soup
Vegetables
4 large potatoes
6 medium carrots
1 pint home canned wax beans or 1 can peas

Roll cracker crumbs fine, cut onion in small pieces. Add these to beef, egg, milk and salt. Mix and make into small rolls as long as a finger or 2½ inches long and 1 inch or so thick. Brown carefully in skillet with fat. If tomato soup is thick it should be made thin with the water which will be drained from the vegetables as they are cooked. The meat and thin tomato soup should be allowed to simmer a bit in a large kettle. Prepare carrots. Allow to boil 10 minutes. Add prepared potatoes. Cook in clear salted water until done, drain and add to the prepared meat and gravy. Add the beans or peas and heat all together. This is delicious and a real meat saver.
Mrs. R. Couture

HAMBURG CASSEROLE

Potatoes
Onions, sliced
Rice, cooked
Hamburg steak
Pint cooked tomatoes
Salt
Pepper

Place a layer of sliced raw potatoes in a casserole, then a layer of sliced raw onions. Over this spread a cup of cooked rice, then a layer of Hamburg steak. Now pour in a pint of cooked tomatoes. Season each layer with salt and pepper. Bake 1 hour.

AMERICAN CHOP SUEY

1 cup macaroni
1 pound ground beef, or beef and pork mixed
2 cups celery, cut in small pieces
1 teaspoon salt
1 medium onion, cut fine
2 cups tomatoes

Boil macaroni in salted water until tender. Drain. Mix with the other ingredients. Pour into casserole or baking disk. Cover and bake for 1 hour, or until meat and celery are done. Spaghetti or noodles may be used in place of macaroni.
Mrs. Leonard Otto

ON RAISING OUR CHILDREN

THERE is more to parenthood than simply providing a child with the physical needs of life. There are spiritual needs which must also be met, and God has given an eternal principle to guide us. It is written, "Train up a child in the way he should go: and when he is old, he will not depart from it" (Prov. 22:6).

Many illustrations of the truth of this precept are to be found in the Bible. There is Hannah, for example, the mother of Samuel. She dedicated her son to the Lord before he was born (I Sam. 1:11). More than this, she kept her vow, and her boy became known for the godly life he lived afterward.

When God places a child in a home, He puts a tremendous responsibility on the shoulders of the parents. By the way they bring the little one up, they determine what manner of man he shall be. While they cannot remove all the obstacles from the pathway of their child, they can prepare him to overcome obstacles and emerge victorious from temptation, by raising him in the nurture and admonition of the Lord.

Susanna Wesley was the mother of nineteen children. Some of them died in infancy, but we know that at least thirteen of them survived. Her husband was the Rev. Samuel Wesley, a clergyman of the church of England. They were married in 1689, and two years afterward Mr. Wesley was appointed rector of South Ormsby, at a salary of two hundred fifty dollars a year.

In 1697 the Wesleys moved to the little town of Epworth, and it was here that most of the children were born. At least four of these children became scholars of distinction. With a large family and a small income, the Wesleys were in debt much of their lives. But Susanna Wesley was a woman of strong mind, and she desired for her children a good education, something difficult to secure in those days.

On one occasion Samuel Wesley was thrown into prison because of his inability to pay his debts. It was at this time that Susanna Wesley undertook to manage the financial affairs of her home, as well as the rearing and education of her children.

In spite of poverty, sickness and disappointment, she was an ideal mother. She drew up a set of rules to govern her household, and the family was a happy and harmonious one: a notable accomplishment, in a family of such a size.

The training of her children began almost as soon as they were born. The little children had their own table near to that of the older members of the family so they could be supervised. As soon as a child could handle a knife and fork, he was promoted to the family table. Thus the children were taught the social graces, so lacking in many homes today. They were taught to respect one another also. Mrs. Wesley was firm and patient with them all, but she never lost her temper or scolded.

John Wesley was born a few weeks before his father was cast into a debtor's prison. During this imprisonment, mother Wesley held worship services in her own home. At first only the immediate family and servants attended, but soon the house was overflowing

MARZETTE

8 ounce package of noodles ½ pound ground pork ½ pound ground beef Medium-sized onion, chopped 1 cup celery 1 medium can mushrooms (broken) 1 pint tomato puree	Cook noodles until tender. Drain. Blanch. Fry meat until brown in your favorite shortening. Mix meat and noodles through. Then add vegetables. Put into baking dish. Pour tomato puree over the top and bake 45 minutes in a moderate oven. *Miss Sadie Farner*

RAW POTATO HASH

4 to 6 potatoes 2 cups diced left-over meat 2 tablespoons celery 1 tablespoon green pepper 1 medium-sized onion Salt and pepper	Grind fine the green pepper, celery and onion; simmer in fat until slightly tender. Add ground raw potatoes and cook until slightly brown. Add meat and season to taste. Keep over slow flame for about 12 to 20 minutes, stirring occasionally. *Mrs. Effie Willemin*

SCALLOPED CHICKEN WITH NOODLES

8 ounces egg noodles Chicken	Boil noodles until tender, drain and blanch with cold water. Stew chicken cut into small pieces. You can use left-over chicken. Place in baking dish with alternate layers of boiled noodles. Thicken the broth to a cream with flour and pour over noodles and chicken. Bake about 15 minutes. *Miss Sadie Farner*

CHICKEN LOAF

1 4-5 pound chicken 2 cups bread crumbs ½ cup rice 1 teaspoon salt ¼ cup chopped pimiento 4 well-beaten eggs ¼ cup melted chicken fat, or butter ¾ quart broth Sauce: ¼ cup butter ¼ cup flour 1 pint broth ¼ cup cream ¼ teaspoon salt 2 beaten egg yolks ½ tablespoon lemon juice ¼ teaspoon paprika	Boil the chicken in plenty of water. Cool. Bone it and cut into small pieces. Cook the rice until tender. Drain, and pour cold water over it. Roll the dried bread crumbs. Combine all the ingredients. Bake 1 hour in a 325° F. oven, in a shallow pan. Serve the sauce as gravy with the chicken loaf. Will serve 16 people. *Mrs. John Holland*

ONE DISH MEAL

2 carrots 2 turnips 4 potatoes 1 onion 1 pound sausage	Lay sausage in center of pan, slice the vegetables around the sausage. Pour in a little water. As the sausage begins to cook, break it in pieces with a fork. One cup of tomatoes can be added if desired. Season to taste.

with friends and neighbors.

Mother Wesley was very careful of the spiritual as well as the physical welfare of her family. How important it is for parents to look after the spiritual life of their children instead of depending upon the minister or Sunday School teacher, who has only one or two hours a week to speak to them of the things of God!

Charles Wesley was the seventeenth child in this God-fearing family. He became one of the greatest hymn writers of the age. His hymn, "Jesus, Lover of My Soul," has been a great favorite.

When John Wesley was a very small child, he had an almost miraculous escape from fire when the rectory was burned to the ground. Later his mother wrote, in her book of private meditations, "I do intend to be more particularly careful of the soul of this child that Thou hast so mercifully provided for, than I have ever been, that I may do my best to instill into his mind the principles of Thy true religion and virtue."

When John and Charles had a call to come to America to preach to the settlers here, they were reluctant to come because by this time their mother was well up in years. When they spoke to her about it she said, "Had I twenty sons and knew I should never see any of them again, I would be happy to know they were doing God's will."

Mr. Wesley recognized the gifts and virtues of his wife and at one time he wrote to his eldest son, "Live such a virtuous and religious life that she may find that her love and care have not been lost upon you, but that we may all meet in heaven."

Susanna Wesley died at the age of seventy-four. Her parting words were, "Children, as soon as I am released, sing a song of praise to God."

Augustine, the saintly scholar, was saved because of the constant and fervent prayer of Monica, his Christian mother. His father was a pagan; Augustine inherited many of the evil habits of his father and cultivated others of his own. However, his mother never ceased to pray for him. When he was his worst, she never gave up, but prayed the more for him, until one day she received word that he was saved. What a wonderful day that must have been for her!

Henry Ward Beecher once said, "The mother's heart is the child's schoolroom." How true this is. Behind every great man there is almost always a great mother. Said Abraham Lincoln, "All that I am or hope to be, I owe to my angel mother."

We do not need money, a high social position, or any other advantage, in order to raise a truly Christian family. However, it does take constant communion with God, both in teaching and practice. We cannot expect our children to live a spiritual life if we allow our actions to contradict the high standards we set before them in our teaching from the Bible.

The experience of all the centuries which have passed, and the evidence of our own generation, testify to the truth of the Word of God. "Train up a child in the way he should go; and when he is old, he will not depart from it."

Mrs. Wiley S. Young

27

MEXICAN CHILI CON CARNE

1 pound dry kidney beans (red)
1 pound chopped beef
Small piece of beef suet
1 quart or No. 3 can tomatoes
1 green pepper
1 large onion, or more
2 tablespoons whole mixed spices
½ teaspoon pepper
1 teaspoon or more salt
1 large tablespoon fat

Wash and soak kidney beans in water over night or for several hours. Start to cook slowly in the same water, which should well cover the beans. Add tomatoes, salt, pepper and suet at once. Add the rest of the ingredients as they are prepared. Remove seeds and dice green pepper. Use part of fat to lightly brown diced onion; use the same skillet and the rest of the fat to brown chopped beef. Use a large spoon to keep the beef separated in small pieces. Make a small bag of very thin material and place whole spices in it. Be sure to have a tiny dry red pepper in the spices, if high flavor is desired. Simmer slowly for 2 hours. Add water from time to time to keep ingredients covered. Remove spice bag and particles of suet. The secret of this Mexican dish is in the dry beans and spices for the flavor is cooked through. Cook spaghetti or noodles, drain, add to chili; or serve in a separate dish just as desired.

Mrs. R. Couture

PORK TENDERLOIN IN CASSEROLE

Pork tenderloin
1 tablespoon flour
2 cups milk
Salt
Pepper
Onion juice
Celery salt

Dip in flour and brown in hot pan. Add to the drippings a large tablespoon of flour. Stir until brown. Add milk, salt, pepper, a little onion juice and celery salt. Pour over meat. Bake slowly 2 hours in the oven.

Miss Cleda Smith

PORK CHOPS AND SAUERKRAUT

4 thick pork chops
Flour
3 tablespoons fat
1 onion, sliced
2½ cups sauerkraut
Mashed potatoes

Salt the pork chops and dredge them lightly in flour. Saute them in the hot fat until well browned. Then turn the fat into a baking dish and add the onion, covering it with the sauerkraut. Place the chops on top of the kraut and cover the dish tightly. Bake in a slow oven (300° F.) for 1½ to 2 hours. Cover the chops with a generous layer of fluffy mashed potatoes, increase the heat to 400° F. and bake until the potatoes are lightly browned. Delicious! (A little water may be added if the kraut is not juicy, or is too salty.)

Mrs. Agnes Hammar

CHEESE SOUFFLE

4 tablespoons butter
4 tablespoons flour
1½ cups milk
1 teaspoon salt
Dash of cayenne
½ pound American cheese, sliced
6 eggs

Make a sauce with the butter, flour, milk and seasonings. When thickened and smooth remove from the heat and add the sliced cheese. Stir until the cheese is melted. Add the beaten yolk of eggs and mix well. Cool the mixture, and slowly pour it into the stiffly beaten white of the eggs. Mix carefully but thoroughly. Pour into a 2-quart casserole and bake 1¼ hours in a slow oven (300° F.). Serve at once.

GOD KNOWS

*God of our salvation, who art the confidence of all the ends of the
earth, and of them that are afar off upon the sea.*   (Psalm 65:5)

. . . there go the ships . . . . these all wait upon thee.
(Psalm 104:26, 27)

God made the sea, and by His hand
  Controls the raging wave,
Thus from the dangers of the deep
  Our God has power to save.

God sees the ships of man's design
  Tossed about at will,
He sees from His almighty throne
  The elements that kill.

God knows the hearts that ache today
  For those upon the sea,
He hears the searching cry of those
  Now torn by memory.

God sees, He knows, He hears, He cares
  What happens to His own,
And so your sailor on the sea
  Can never be alone!

Eileen M. Fleeton

❦

*They that go down to the sea in ships, that do business in great
waters, these see the works of the Lord, and his wonders in the
deep. For he commandeth, and raiseth the stormy wind, which
lifteth up the waves thereof. They mount up to the heavens, they
go down again to the depths: their soul is melted because of trouble.
They reel to and fro, and stagger like a drunken man, and are at
their wit's end. Then they cry unto the Lord in their trouble, and
he bringeth them out of their distresses. He maketh the storm a
calm, so that the waves thereof are still. Then are they glad because
they be quiet; so he bringeth them unto their desired haven.*
(Psalm 107:23-30)

SCALLOPED POTATOES with SALT PORK and HERRING (Finnish)

5 medium-sized potatoes
2 tablespoons flour
4 tablespoons butter
Salt and pepper
¼ pound salt pork in small pieces
1 salt herring in small pieces
Water

Peel potatoes and slice thin. Arrange a layer in a buttered casserole. Sprinkle with salt and pepper, flour and bits of butter, over which sprinkle a few pieces of salt pork. Then add another layer of the potato and seasoning as before, substituting the salt herring for the pork in the second layer. Add the remaining potatoes, seasoning them, combine the salt pork and herring and cover with a thin layer of potatoes, and add water till it shows between the slices of potato. Cover and bake at 350°-400° F. for 1 to 1½ hours, until potatoes are tender. Remove the cover for the last 15 minutes to brown the top. Serve from baking dish. Will serve 5 or 6.
Mrs. Gertrude Hansen

HAM RING

1 pound ground ham
1 pound ground beef or pork
½ teaspoon salt
2 cups milk
½ cup tapioca
1 teaspoon Worcestershire sauce
Minced onion (optional)

Mix well and bake 1 hour in a ring mold. Serve with escalloped potatoes in center of mold. Or serve hot potato salad in center.
L. Bourne

CHILI CON CARNE

1½ pound hamburger
1 No. 2½ can tomatoes
1 package elbow macaroni
1 No. 2 can brown beans
3 to 4 onions
Salt and pepper
Pinch of chili powder

Brown the onions in butter, and add the hamburger. Cook through. Add the macaroni which has been cooked slightly, and then add tomatoes, beans and seasoning. Simmer for about 1½ hours.
Mrs. Ivar Hallquist

RUSSIAN FLUFF

¾ pound ground meat
1 teaspoon salt
Dash of pepper
1 cup celery
1 onion, cut fine
¾ cup rice
1 can corn
1 can tomato soup
Crumbs
Bacon

Simmer together the seasoned meat, celery and onion. Put the mixture in greased casserole, over this pour the boiled rice. Then add a can of corn and over this pour the tomato soup. Cover with crumbs and bacon cut in 2-inch pieces.
Mrs. G. Kuiper

MACARONI HAM CASSEROLE

1 inch slice ham
1 package macaroni broken
3 cups tomato juice
½ cup tomato catsup
1 No. 2½ can tomatoes
Salt and pepper
½ cup grated cheese
1 green pepper

Put ham in bottom of deep baking dish. Add macaroni and pour on tomato juice, catsup and tomatoes. Sprinkle with salt and pepper. Cover with cheese; decorate with green pepper rings. Cover and bake 45 minutes in moderate oven, (350° F.). Uncover and bake 15 minutes more.
Mrs. Maurice Olson

Nothing lies beyond the reach of prayer except that which lies outside the will of God.

❦

LIFE'S COMMON THINGS

I thank Thee, Lord, that I can see—
For some cannot—the circling bee,
The smile of a friend, the sun-stained west,
For sight and sound and night-long rest,
Ears hearing the creek's cool call and song,
Slipping and slapping its way along:
    For these let me thank Thee, Lord.

For baking spices, for earth's sweet smell,
For fresh-dried clothes—the odors that swell
My heart with their fragrance. Then let me taste
And touch, dear Lord. Let me not waste
A single blessing by senses grasped.
Head bowed in gratitude, hands clasped,
    For all these I praise Thee, Lord.

I thank Thee, Lord, for my little son.
Weary of work, my tasks undone—
Panting he came, arms loaded, he stood,
"See, Mother, I love you; I brought you some wood."
So naughty that day, then thus he came
A blessing from Thee—oh, this my shame,
    Should I fail to thank Thee, Lord.

For husband's love, a baby to share—
Caring for her, teach me Thy care
And love for me, much greater than mine.
In Thy blest work, make my lips Thine
To tell some soul of Thy loving grace,
Show him to paths that seek Thy face
    That we two may thank Thee, Lord.

Gretta M. Van Duken, Moody Monthly

VEGETABLE COOKERY

Vegetables should be fresh, firm and ripe. Do not buy vegetables that are old, withered, moldy or bruised, under ripe, or over ripe; there is no saving in cost from purchasing such vegetables. Head vegetables should be solid, with few waste leaves. Cauliflower should be white and firm, with no blemishes. Leafy vegetables should be crisp. Peas and beans should have crisp pods. Buy vegetables of medium size and regular shape. The first essential for all vegetable cookery is a fairly heavy saucepan with a tightly fitting cover.

Vegetables should be cooked over *low* heat in *very little* water, and a tightly fitting cover keeps the steam in so they cook thoroughly without boiling dry.

Green, leafy vegetables like spinach and kale do not need *any* water—there should be plenty clinging to the leaves after washing. So simply press the greens down into the pan and sprinkle with equal amounts of sugar and salt . . . about a teaspoon of each to a pound and a half of greens.

Cover tightly and put over medium heat until the juices start to boil, then **reduce** the heat as much as possible.

Spinach will be cooked in ten minutes, but kale will take about twenty-five minutes, depending on how young and tender it is.

Drain off any liquid and save it. Use it for vegetable soups or put it in the refrigerator and serve it half with tomato juice . . . it's delicious that way.

Chop the greens before serving and season just as carefully as you would a sauce, adding additional salt and pepper and butter to taste . . . there are lots of garnishes too, like tiny diced beets or chopped hard boiled egg . . . but right now we're mainly concerned with cooking the vegetables . . . the rest is a matter of preference and entirely up to you.

And now for the other kinds of vegetables . . . carrots . . . string beans . . . lima beans . . . Brussels sprouts . . . and so forth.

They can all be cooked in exactly the same simple way . . . but with these non-*leafy* and consequently less *juicy* vegetables, you will have to put a tiny bit of water in the bottom of the pan to start with. Just enough to *cover* the bottom . . . about one-quarter of an inch deep . . . and *no more*. Shred cabbage, coarsely . . . dice carrots and white turnips . . . and slice string beans lengthwise . . . sprinkle all vegetables with sugar as well as salt, and cook tightly covered for ten to fifteen minutes.

It is *over*-cooking that *develops* strong flavors in Brussels sprouts, broccoli and cabbage. Broccoli, cooked in the tiniest amount of water and seasoned with sugar as well as salt, is wonderfully delicate in flavor . . . and especially good to serve cold as a luncheon salad.

The addition of sugar during cooking has a great deal to do with it too, for sugar brings out the naturally sweet flavor of all vegetables beautifully . . . in just exactly the same way that it improves the flavor of all fruits.

SWEET POTATO SURPRISE

Mash and season to taste with salt and pepper one can sweet potatoes. Form into balls placing in center of each a marshmallow. Roll in cracker or toast crumbs. Place in baking dish and pour melted butter over balls. Brown in oven just before serving.

Mrs. Larry Larson

ARE YOU A WILTED LEAF OF LETTUCE?

Place a leaf of lettuce under the faucet. Turn the hot water upon it and watch it shrivel and shrink. Reach for the cold faucet and see the way the leaf of lettuce will wriggle and try to smile.

Our mind has two such faucets. We can turn on the heat of self-pity, anger, envy, resentment, spite, jealousy, revenge, or hate, and our souls will shrivel and pucker. Unkind words will come to our lips and bring unhappiness to us and those around us. Or we may turn on refreshing thoughts of love, duty, honor, sharing, kindness, and bring laughter and joy to those near us and to ourselves.

How can I think kind thoughts of one who has done me a wrong? Remember "a soft answer turneth away wrath." Substitute bitter thoughts to thoughts of hope for his success, his happiness. Or stop entirely all thoughts concerning him or the events which caused unhappiness, and begin to think how to make some one else happy as a recompense. How can I think healthy thoughts when I am sick? By knowing that God is near at hand, ready to have you "Knock and it shall be opened unto you," and by keeping your thoughts uplifted you help Him to aid you to get well.

Don't wilt yourself. Be what God intended you to be. Turn on the right faucet.

Mary B. Steyle
Gospel Herald

❧

THINGS YOU JUST CAN'T DO

Sow bad habits and reap good character.
Sow jealousy and hatred and reap love and friendship.
Sow dissipation and reap a healthy body.
Sow deception and reap confidence.
Sow cowardice and reap courage.
Sow neglect of the Bible and reap a well-guided life.

❧

As objects close to the eye shut out larger objects on the horizon, so man sometimes covers up the entire disc of eternity with a dollar, and quenches transcendent glories with a little shining dust.

E. H. Chapin

33

VEGETABLE LUNCHEON PLATE

½ pound American cheese
⅓ cup milk
1 cauliflower
Broiled tomato halves
Hot buttered whole green beans
Pimiento strips

Melt the cheese in the top of a double boiler. Add the milk gradually, stirring constantly until the sauce is smooth.

Cook the whole cauliflower, drain well and place it in the center of a round chop plate. Pour the hot sauce over it, and surround it with broiled tomato halves and fagots of the green beans garnished with pimiento strips.

VEGETABLE PARTY-PIE

PASTRY (2-crust recipe)
3 tablespoons butter or margarine
3 tablespoons flour
1 ½ cups milk
½ pound American cheese, shredded
Salt, pepper
½ teaspoon dry mustard
1 ½ cups cooked peas
½ cup cooked small whole onions
1 cup cooked sliced celery

Line a round shallow baking dish (8½ x 2 inches) with pastry. Roll out the remaining pastry, cut it into a circle a little smaller than the baking dish. Place on a baking sheet and cut into three pie-shaped pieces. Decorate the center of each by cutting out part of the pastry with a fancy cutter. Bake these pieces and the pastry shell in a hot oven (425° F.) 15 minutes, or until lightly browned.

Make cream sauce with the butter or margarine, flour, and milk. Add the shredded cheese and stir until it is melted. Add seasonings, and the peas, onions and celery. Pour into the baked shell, cover with the pastry cut-outs, and place in a moderate oven to heat through. Garnish with parsley.

SCALLOPED ASPARAGUS

4 tablespoons butter
¼ cup flour
1 cup milk
Also liquid from asparagus
4 hard boiled eggs

In a greased casserole put half of asparagus and 4 hard boiled eggs on top. Then a layer of cream sauce, and grated cheese. On top layer put bread crumbs. Dress with asparagus tips. Brown in hot oven 20 minutes.

Mrs. Wallace Samuelson

ASPARAGUS TIMBALES

2 tablespoons butter or margarine
¼ cup flour
1 teaspoon salt
½ cup bread crumbs
3 eggs (beaten)
⅓ teaspoon paprika
1 cup milk
1 ½ cups diced, cooked or canned asparagus

Melt the butter or margarine, add the flour and seasonings and gradually the milk to make a sauce. Stir in the asparagus, bread and eggs. Transfer to oiled cups or a mold. Stand in a pan of hot water and bake until firm like a custard.

Mrs. Eldon A. Larson

RUTABAGA

Cut rutabaga into ½-inch cubes. Boil in salted water until done. Drain immediately and add enough cream to cover. Add 2 tablespoons butter. Cook slowly until thick, or about ½ hour.

Mrs. Harold E. Nelson

CHEESE SOUFFLE, See Page 28

Courtesy Kraft Cheese Co.

Courtesy The Quaker Oats Co. **SPAGHETTI RING WITH ASPARAGUS AND EGGS, See Page 36** ➡

◄ **VEGETABLE LUNCHEON**, See Page 34

Courtesy Kraft Cheese Co.

Courtesy Kraft Cheese Co.

VEGETABLE PARTY- PIE, See Page 34

THE LITTLE TASKS

The ceaseless round of little things
Which every dawning morning brings—
'Tis this, which makes my sum of care
'Tis this, I pray for strength to bear.
Lord, help me through it all to see
How much my duties bring to me.

These never ending tasks I face
Which sometimes seem so commonplace—
The beds I make to make again,
The little windows splashed with rain,
The floors I sweep, the chairs I dust,—
All these I do because I must.

The little garments I repair
And make them fit once more to wear,
The meals I get, the rows and rows
Of dishes every woman knows;
'Tis these, dear Lord, that make me doubt
And fear they'll wear my patience out.

Lord, keep my vision sweet and clear
When irksome days grow dark and drear;
Still let me see their eyes aglow
With love that shall be mine to know;
Help me to sing each morning through,
Because such tasks are mine to do.

For them I sew, for them I bake,
For them these endless pains I take;
Help me to see in all I touch
The little hearts I love so much,
And understand ('tis all I ask)
The meaning of each little task.

Edgar A. Guest
Copyrighted. Used by permission of
The Reilly & Lee Co., Chicago, Ill.

SPAGHETTI RING WITH ASPARAGUS AND EGGS
(Serves 6)

1 package spaghetti
1 cup cooked ground beef liver
½ clove garlic (chopped)
2 tablespoons pimiento (chopped)
½ teaspoon salt
¼ teaspoon pepper
2 eggs (beaten)
¾ cup coffee cream

Filling:

2 tablespoons butter
2 tablespoons flour
1 ½ cups milk
½ teaspoon salt
¼ teaspoon pepper
1 cup cooked asparagus (cut)
2 hard-cooked eggs (sliced)

Break spaghetti and cook until tender in 2 quarts boiling water to which 1 tablespoon salt has been added. Drain and add to it the ground liver, garlic, pimiento, salt, pepper, eggs and cream. Pour into buttered ring mold, place in shallow pan of hot water, and bake at moderate temperature (350° F.) for about one hour.

To make the filling, melt the butter in a saucepan and add flour. Blend thoroughly and then add milk. Cook, stirring constantly, until mixture thickens. Add seasonings and lightly stir in the asparagus. Fill center of spaghetti mold with creamed asparagus and top with slices of hard-cooked eggs.

BAKED BEANS

1 pound beans
Small bottle catsup
½ teaspoon mustard
⅛ cup sugar
¼ teaspoon pepper
3 tablespoons vinegar
Small piece salt pork

Boil beans until soft. Add other ingredients. Fry salt pork and place on top. Pour fat over top and bake in oven for about one hour. The beans should be very moist (completely covered) when put in the oven.

Mrs. Martin Crook

SPANISH CHEESE LIMAS

½ cup chopped onion
1 cup chopped celery
2 cups canned tomatoes (drained)
1 ½ teaspoons salt
⅛ teaspoon pepper
Dash of cayenne
2 teaspoons Worcestershire sauce
2 cups canned lima beans or 1 box frosted limas, cooked
1 ½ cups grated American cheese

Brown onion and celery lightly in butter, and combine with tomatoes, seasonings, Worcestershire sauce and limas. Cook slowly 20 minutes, stirring occasionally. Alternate layers of lima bean mixture and cheese in buttered casserole. Bake in moderate oven 350° F. 30 minutes. Serves 6.

Mrs. Milton Bloom

SCALLOPED POTATOES

2 tablespoons grated cheese
3 tablespoons butter
1 teaspoon salt
2 tablespoons flour
¼ teaspoon paprika
¼ teaspoon pepper
1 ½ cups milk
6 large potatoes
1 green pepper

Put cheese and butter in a saucepan. When melted, add flour, salt, paprika and pepper. Cook until smooth and creamy. Add milk slowly, stirring until well blended. Cook until thickened. Pare potatoes and slice rather thin. Chop the pepper. Put a layer of potatoes in a greased casserole and sprinkle with chopped pepper. Add another layer of potatoes and so on until dish is filled. Over all pour the cheese sauce. Dot with butter. Bake in oven (350° F.).

Mrs. Walter Carlson

PRAYER TIME

The while she darns the children's socks,
    She prays for little stumbling feet;
Each folded pair within its box
    Fits faith's bright sandals, sure and fleet.

While washing out, with mother pains,
    Small, dusty suits, and frocks, and slips,
She prays that God may cleanse the stains
    From little hands, and hearts, and lips.

And when she breaks the fragrant bread,
    Or pours a portion in each cup,
For grace to keep their spirits fed
    Her mother-heart is lifted up.

O busy ones, whose souls grow faint,
    Whose tasks seem longer than the day,
It doesn't take a cloistered saint
    To find a little time to pray.

Ruby Weyburn Tobias
Sunday School Times

❧

HEARTS FOUND IN THE BIBLE

Broken Heart — Psalm 34:18—"The Lord is nigh unto them that are of a *broken* heart; and saveth such as be of a contrite spirit."

Clean Heart — Psalm 51:10—"Create in me a *clean* heart, O God; and renew a right spirit within me."

Deceitful Heart — Prov. 12:20—"*Deceit* is in the heart of them that imagine evil: but to the counsellors of peace is joy."

Blind Heart — Eph. 4:17, 18—"This I say, therefore, and testify in the Lord, that ye henceforth walk not as other Gentiles walk in the vanity of their mind, Having the understanding darkened, being alienated from the life of God through the ignorance that is in them, because of the *blindness* of their heart."

Froward Heart — Prov. 17:20—"He that hath a *froward* heart findeth no good; and he that hath a perverse tongue falleth into mischief."

Foolish Heart — Prov. 15:7—"The lips of the wise disperse knowledge: but the heart of the *foolish* doeth not so."

GLAZED SWEET POTATOES

Sweet potatoes
½ cup sugar
4 tablespoons water
1 tablespoon butter

Pare desired quantity of potatoes. Cut in half lengthwise. Put in buttered pan or baking dish, and pour over them the syrup (sugar, water and butter) which has been boiled for 3 minutes. Bake covered.

Mrs. Doris Landers

SWEET POTATO BALLS

2 cups mashed sweet potatoes
3 tablespoons butter
½ teaspoon salt
Few grains pepper
1 beaten egg

To the mashed sweet potatoes add the butter, salt, pepper and egg. Shape in small balls. Roll in crushed corn flakes. Fry in deep fat and drain. If potatoes are very dry it will be necessary to add hot milk to moisten.

Mrs. Irving Swanson

HARVARD BEETS

1 No. 2 can diced beets
½ cup sugar
½ tablespoon cornstarch
½ cup vinegar

Mix sugar and cornstarch, add vinegar and let boil for five minutes. Drain the beets, and pour the mixture over them. Let stand about ½ hour; just before serving add 2 tablespoons butter.

Mrs. Willard Lundin

COOKED RED CABBAGE

1 tablespoon butter
1 tablespoon lard
3 tablespoons sugar, salt and pepper
1 large apple, cut up
8 tablespoons vinegar
Red cabbage

Shred the cabbage, add to the other ingredients, and cook. A little water may be added, but it is better if it is cooked without. Watch it carefully so it won't burn. About an hour before it is done, add the vinegar.

Mrs. John Holland

CARROT LOAF

2 cups cooked carrots (diced or mashed)
¾ cup soft bread crumbs
1⅓ cups milk
½ teaspoon salt
½ cup grated cheese
4 tablespoons melted butter
4 eggs

Soak crumbs in heated milk. Add salt, butter, cheese, slightly beaten egg yolks and carrots. Fold in stiffly beaten egg whites. Bake in well greased casserole in moderate oven (375° F.) about 45 minutes or until firm. Serve with a cheese or vegetable sauce.

Mrs. Gust Carlson

FRESH CORN PUDDING

6 large, or 8 small ears of corn
2 eggs, beaten light
1 tablespoon grated onion
2 tablespoons minced green pepper
1 tablespoon butter
¾ teaspoon salt
⅛ teaspoon black pepper
1 tablespoon sugar
⅞ cup milk

Scrape the kernels from the ears of corn. Add the eggs to the corn. Stir in the grated onion, the minced green peppers which have been sauteed in 1 tablespoon butter, the salt, pepper and sugar. Add the milk, and pour the mixture into a buttered baking dish. Bake the pudding in a moderate oven (350° F.) for 45 minutes. serve as soon as possible after removal from oven.

Mrs. Doris Landers

Glad Heart	Psalm 4:7—"Thou hast put *gladness* in my heart."
Merry Heart	Prov. 15:13—"A *merry* heart maketh a cheerful countenance; but by sorrow of the heart the spirit is broken."
Perfect Heart	I Kings 9:61—"Let your heart therefore be *perfect* with the Lord our God, to walk in His statutes, and to keep His commandments."
Perverse Heart	Prov. 12:8—"A man shall be commended according to his wisdom: but he that is of a *perverse* heart shall be despised."
Proud Heart	Prov. 16:5—"Every one that is *proud* in heart is an abomination to the Lord."
Pure Heart	Psalm 24:4—"Who shall ascend into the hill of the Lord? or who shall stand in His holy place? He that hath clean hands and a *pure* heart."
Rejoicing Heart	Psalm 105:3—"Glory ye in His holy name: let the heart of them *rejoice* that seek the Lord." Psalm 19:8—"The statutes of the Lord are right, *rejoicing* the heart; the commandment of the Lord is pure, enlightening the eyes."
Righteous Heart	Prov. 15:28—"The *heart of the righteous* studieth to answer, but the mouth of the wicked poureth out evil things."
Tender Heart	Eph. 4:32—"And be ye kind one to another, *tenderhearted*, forgiving one another, even as God for Christ's sake hath forgiven you."
Sick Heart	Prov. 13:12—"Hope deferred maketh the *heart sick:* but when the desire cometh, it is a tree of life."
Sound Heart	Prov. 14:30—"A *sound* heart is the life of the flesh: but envy the rottenness of the bones."
Understanding Heart	I Kings 3:11, 12—"Because thou hast asked not for thyself long life; neither hast asked riches for thyself, nor hast asked the life of thine enemies, but hast asked for thyself understanding to discern judgment, Behold, I have done according to thy words: lo, I have given thee a wise and an *understanding* heart."
Upright Heart	Psalm 7:10—"My defense is of God, which saveth the *upright* in heart."
Wise Heart	Prov. 10:8—"The *wise* in heart will receive commandments: but a prating fool shall fail."
Willing Heart	Exodus 35:5—"Whatsoever is of a *willing* heart, let him bring it, an offering to the Lord; gold, and silver and brass."

SALADS

Jellied desserts and salads are the perfect way to get those fresh fruits and vegetables into the family diet.

Color is always important, especially in the springtime . . . and it so happens that color is the very best guide to successful combinations of either fruits or vegetables.

Leave the bright red peel on diced apples if you like, and remember that carrots, beets, green peppers and raw spinach leaves add lots of color to vegetable combinations.

Plain unflavored gelatine makes the very nicest salads and desserts of all because the fresh fruit juice you use makes a world of difference in flavor . . . to say nothing of vitamins.

When you make molded vegetable salads save every drop of water left from vegetable cookery. There shouldn't be much, of course, but even if it's only a tablespoon or two, save it . . . It's just full of delicious flavor, let alone those vitamins and minerals. So use it in the measured cup of hot liquid that you need.

Basic recipe that can be used for any combination of either fruits or vegetables.

Empty an envelope of plain gelatine into a quarter cup of cold water. Let the gelatine soften in the water for about five minutes then dissolve the softened gelatine completely in one cup of hot water . . . or fruit or vegetable juice.

Add three tablespoons of lemon juice (or vinegar is nice with a vegetable salad if you have vegetable liquid in the hot water) . . . then add a quarter cup of sugar and a quarter teaspoon of salt.

Stir thoroughly, then let it cool. When the mixture starts to thicken fold in one and a half cups of diced fresh fruits or vegetables, and chill in a mold until serving time.

COMBINATIONS FOR SALADS

These fruits and vegetables are tasty salad combinations:

FRUITS

Apples, celery, raisins, dates.
Pineapples, marshmallows, nuts.
Pineapple, grapefruit, nuts.
Oranges, bananas, dates.
Apples, pineapple, dates.
Pears, pineapple, cherries.
Apples, celery, nuts.
White cherries, celery, nuts.

VEGETABLES

One part peas, three parts salmon.
Salmon, onions, pickles; garnish with hard boiled eggs.
Meat, pickles, celery, mayonnaise.
Potatoes, celery, onion, peas, chopped beets; parsley garnish.
Carrots, celery, raisins.
Shredded cabbage, nuts, celery, apples.

"TOSSED" SALAD

Greens
½ cucumber
Radishes
Tomato
French dressing

Into a salad bowl toss all the crisp greens you can lay your hands on. Leaf lettuce, shredded with a pair of scissors, tender leaves of water cress and celery leaves will do nicely by themselves; add ½ cucumber, diced, a few radishes and a tomato. Toss lightly with a thin French dressing. Serve immediately.

Mrs. Doris Landers

"IF" FOR GIRLS
(With apologies to Kipling)

If you can fill life full of wholesome pleasure,
    Yet not make fun your only end and aim;
If you can row and swim, play golf and tennis,
    And yet keep sweet and girlish just the same;
If you can lead your class in school or college
    And yet not feel that you have learned it all;
Or, being slow, see others pass above you,
    Rejoice with them, yet not feel that you're small;

If you can like the boys and win their favor,
    Yet not one minute lose your self-respect;
But make each one you talk with feel the stronger
    And glad to live the life that you expect;
If you can dress in style and be attractive
    Yet do not think that clothes count more than brains;
If you can mix with those of wealth and culture,
    Yet see that simple courtesy remains;

If you can meet with heartaches and keep cheery,
    Have discouragements, yet rise above them all;
If daily you can make the world the better,
    Bring cheer to lonely hearts and help to all;
If you can win the love of little children
    And help to keep their lives sweet, pure and true—
You'll grow to splendid womanhood, my dear one,
    And be of service, whatso'er you do.

Ina Hogg
Girlhood Days

৵৵৵

God sends us no trial, whether great or small, without first preparing us. Trials are God's vote of confidence in us. Many a trifling event is sent to test us, ere a greater trial is permitted to break on our heads. We are set to climb the lower peaks before urged to the loftiest summits, with their virgin snows; are made to run with the footmen, before contending with horses; are taught to wade in the shallows, before venturing into the swell of the ocean waves.

F. B. Meyer

FRUIT SALAD BOWL (Serves 4)

8 slices of orange
4 slices of unpeeled red-skinned apple, each "sandwiched" between 2 orange slices
4 crescents of calavo, sprinkled with lemon juice to prevent discoloration
4 long banana slices, sprinkled with lemon juice
Watermelon balls
Whole, unhulled strawberries
Wedge of cantaloupe

Wash and dry carefully one or more varieties of fresh crisp greens such as romaine, lettuce, watercress, endive, chicory, escarole. Arrange attractively in a salad bowl. Place on the greens in definite groups.

Arrange fruit to give good contrast in color, texture and shape. Add French dressing just before serving. In serving see that each one receives a portion of each fruit.

DELICIOUS FRUIT SALAD

1 No. 2 can fruit cocktail
2 slices pineapple, cut up
2 bananas, cut up
6 or 8 marshmallows, cut up
1 cup dressing
1 cup whipped cream

SAUCE:

½ cup butter
½ cup sugar
1 tablespoon flour
1 egg
½ cup whipped cream
⅓ cup pineapple juice

Combine the ingredients. When frozen, this salad can be used as a dessert.

Boil together the pineapple juice, butter, sugar, flour and egg until it begins to thicken. When cool, fold in whipped cream. Fold this into the fruit. Very delicious.

Mrs. Elmer Kinney

SALMON SALAD

½ cup cooked elbow macaroni
1 cup peas
½ cup diced celery
2 tablespoons minced onions
½ cup diced cucumber
2 diced sweet pickles
4 tablespoons minced green pepper
1½ cups salmon, boned and flaked
4 diced tomatoes
2 teaspoons salt
French dressing
Mayonnaise

Combine ingredients in order listed. Blend well. Pile onto a platter. Garnish with lettuce leaves, sliced tomatoes and gherkins, or olives. To decorate the lettuce leaf, dip the edge of it in a plate of paprika. Serves 8-10.

Mrs. Louise Hill

PARTY CHICKEN SALAD

1½ cups cubed canned pineapple
3 ripe bananas, cubed
1½ or 2 cups diced chicken
½ cup finely chopped celery
¼ teaspoon salt

Mix pineapple with bananas to keep from discoloration. Dilute mayonnaise with pineapple juice or cream to right consistency. Use dressing sparingly and mix lightly with ingredients. Serve on crisp greens, garnish with whole almonds or any chopped nuts.

Mrs. H. C. Babel

COTTAGE CHEESE SALAD

Courtesy Bowman Dairy Co.

Courtesy Kraft Cheese Co.

MACEDOINE VEGETABLE SALAD, See Page 44 ➡

CREAM CHEESE CUCUMBER RING, See Page 46

Courtesy Kraft Cheese Co.

Courtesy California Fruit Growers Exchange

FRUIT SALAD BOWL, See Page 42

WHEN LINCOLN PRAYED

"THE HIGH-WATER MARK of the War between the States."
With reverence we read the words; and with quickened pulses we
look from our vantage point on Cemetery Ridge over the meadows
and woodlands of Gettysburg toward Seminary Ridge, for in imagination we see Pickett's men in gray sweep forward in one of the
most colorful and courageous charges recorded in the annals of
men. Long years since the Blue and the Gray have become brothers
again; and to their children, from North and South alike, Gettysburg with its fields and hills, where the fate of the Republic hung
in the balance that July afternoon of 1863, has become a shrine
where anew we dedicate ourselves in devotion. General Daniel E.
Sickles has recorded for us this intimate revelation from the heart
of the Great Emancipator. The General had been severely wounded
on July 2 and after suffering the amputation of a leg, was removed
to Washington where he was visited by the President. We quote
from General Sickles:

"Mr. Lincoln, we heard at Gettysburg that here at the Capital
you were all so anxious about the result of the battle that the
Government officials packed up and got ready to leave at short
notice with the official archives."

"Yes," he said, "some precautions were prudently taken, but,
for my part, I was sure of our success at Gettysburg."

"Why," I asked, "were you so confident? The Army of the
Potomac had suffered many reverses."

There was a pause. The President seemed in deep meditation.
His pale face was lighted up by an expression I had not observed
before. Turning to me he said:

"When Lee crossed the Potomac and entered Pennsylvania
followed by our Army, I felt that the crisis had come. I knew that
defeat in a great battle on Northern soil involved the loss of Washington, to be followed, perhaps, by the intervention of England and
France in favor of the Southern Confederacy. I went to my room
and got down on my knees in prayer. Never before had I prayed
with so much earnestness. I wish I could repeat my prayer. I felt
that I must put all my trust in Almighty God. He gave our people
the best country ever given to man. He alone could save it from
destruction. I had tried my best to do my duty and found myself
unequal to the task. The burden was more than I could bear. God

MACEDOINE VEGETABLE SALAD

Lettuce
Cooked peas
Cooked cauliflower
Cooked green beans
Sliced tomatoes
Watercress
Radish roses
Hard-cooked egg slices
French dressing, or salad dressing

Line a salad bowl with crisp lettuce. In separate lettuce cups put generous portions of peas, cauliflower flowerets, Julienne green beans and sliced tomatoes. Place these filled lettuce cups around the rim of the bowl and fill the center with watercress. Garnish with radish roses and hard-cooked egg slices, and serve with French dressing or salad dressing.

MOLDED BEET SALAD

1 package lemon gelatine
1 package cream cheese
½ cup shredded cabbage
½ cup chopped beets
1 tablespoon minced onion
  (optional)

Dissolve ½ package of gelatine in 1 cup of hot water. Into this mix the cream cheese. Dissolve remaining gelatine and into this mix the shredded cabbage, chopped beets and minced onion; combine and let set.

CARROT SALAD

1 cup chopped celery
1 cup chopped raw carrots
Salt
Pepper
Small amount of sugar
½ cup English walnut meats
½ cup mayonnaise
1 cup whipped cream

Combine the celery and carrots. Add the seasoning and sugar. Add the nutmeats. Mix the mayonnaise and whipped cream, and combine with the other ingredients. Serve on individual salad plates garnished with a spoonful of whipped cream, topped with a nutmeat or candied cherry.

Mrs. Dora Stonestreet

BOWL SLAW

¾ cup chopped bacon cracklings
2 tablespoons lemon juice
1 teaspoon salt
½ teaspoon mustard
½ cup mayonnaise
4 tablespoons green pepper,
  chopped
2 cups, or 1 pound cabbage,
  shredded fine
2 tablespoons parsley
4 tablespoons onion, chopped

Place chopped bacon in pan and fry to golden color. Add lemon juice, salt and mustard. Stir well and mix with mayonnaise. Toss finely chopped vegetables lightly together with mixed dressing. Serve in a large bowl. Serves six.

Mrs. Louise Hill

PINEAPPLE CHEESE SALAD

1 package lime gelatine
1 cup crushed pineapple
½ cup finely chopped celery
1 3-ounce cake Philadelphia
  cream cheese
½ pint whipping cream

Prepare the gelatine. When it is slightly thickened, add the pineapple and celery. Mix thoroughly; then add cheese and cream which have been whipped together. Turn into mold. Chill until firm, then unmold on crisp lettuce. Garnish with whipped cream to which a little mayonnaise has been added. For Christmas it makes a pretty salad if a maraschino cherry is put on top of each dish of salad.

Mrs. LaMar Kiefer

had often been our Protector in other days. I prayed that He would not let the nation perish. I asked Him to help us and give us the victory now.

"I felt that my prayer was answered. I knew that God was on our side. I had no misgivings about the result of Gettysburg."

President Lincoln, like the Samaritan of old, remembered to return thanksgiving unto the Almighty, and on July 15 he issued the following Proclamation:

"It has pleased Almighty God to hearken to the supplication and prayers of an afflicted people, and to vouchsafe to the Army and Navy of the United States victories on land and on sea so signal and so effective as to furnish reasonable grounds for augmented confidence that the union of these States will be maintained, their Constitution preserved, and their peace and prosperity permanently restored. But these victories have been accorded not without sacrifice of life, limb, health, and liberty, incurred by brave, loyal, and patriotic citizens. Domestic affliction in every part of the country follows in the train of these fearful bereavements. It is meet and right to recognize and confess the presence of the Almighty Father and the power of His hand equally in these triumphs and in these sorrows.

"Now, therefore, be it known that I do set apart Thursday, the sixth day of August next, to be observed as a day for national thanksgiving, praise, and prayer.

"Our fathers have labored and died, and we, their children, are entered into the heritage of a united and powerful nation. And shall we not like them, in our hour of national and international distress, seek, President and people alike, the forgiveness, the mercy, and the aid of the God of our fathers?"

Dr. V. Raymond Edman,
Pres. Wheaton College

❧

There's a fight to be fought, there's a work to be done,
And a foe to be met ere the set of the sun;
And the call has gone out o'er the land far and wide,
Who'll follow the banner? Who's on the Lord's side?

45

CREAM CHEESE CUCUMBER RING

2 tablespoons gelatine
¼ cup cold water
½ cup boiling water
¼ cup sugar
½ teaspoon salt
2 tablespoons lemon juice
1 teaspoon scraped onion
1 cup grated drained cucumber
3 3-ounce packages cream cheese
Canned pears
¼ pound red cinnamon candy
Lettuce

Soften the gelatine in the cold water; dissolve it in the boiling water; add the sugar; cool. Add the salt, lemon juice, onion and cucumber. Soften the cream cheese with ¼ cup of the gelatine mixture. Chill the remaining gelatine until partially thickened, then beat it with a dover beater until foamy. Combine with the cheese mixture, pour into a ring mold, and chill until firm.

Let the pears stand an hour in a syrup made by heating the pear juice sufficiently to dissolve the cinnamon candy in it.

Unmold the Cucumber Ring on a chop plate, fill the center with lettuce, and garnish the plate with the pears in crisp lettuce cups.
Serves 5.

CRANBERRY SALAD (Popular Canadian Recipe)

2 pounds cranberries
1 pint water
Sugar to taste
1 cup sliced bananas
1 cup oranges, cut small
1 cup diced pineapple
¼ cup nuts

Cook the cranberries with the water. When tender, rub through sieve and add sugar to taste. When ready to serve add the other ingredients, which must be prepared when wanted, or the bananas will be soft. It does not congeal, nor is it supposed to. However, be careful not to have the cranberry mixture too thin. Try it; you'll love it if you do. This recipe has been handed down from ancestors in Canada.

Mrs. H. J. Boyd

CHRISTMAS CRANBERRY SALAD

1 pound bright red cranberries
1 small orange
2 cups sugar
1 package lemon or lime gelatine
1 pint warm water
1 cup nut meats
1 cup marshmallows
1 cup celery hearts
1 cup ripe apple
Canned pineapple, if desired

Grind the cranberries and orange. Add the sugar, mix and let stand overnight. Dissolve the gelatine in water, and when half set add to first mixture. Add the nutmeats, the marshmallows cut in pieces, the chopped celery hearts, and the apple. Add the pineapple, if desired. Pour into mold and set in a cold place until wanted. Serve in slices or individual molds with whipped cream and thin crosswise slices of maraschino cherries, with cream showing through the center. It's delicious! It may be served with salad dressing, instead of the cream. This is a large recipe, making enough for all the family at Christmas time.

Mrs. Leslie Scott

CHRISTMAS SALAD

1 package lime gelatine
1 cup boiling water
1 cup cold water or fruit syrup
Canned pear halves
Maraschino cherries

Dissolve gelatine in boiling water. Add cold water or syrup from canned pears. Cool. When partially set, pour half of mixture into a ring mold. Arrange pear halves end to end in mold, placing maraschino cherries between halves. Pour over this the remainder of the gelatine. When firmly set, turn out onto salad plate. Garnish with lettuce and maraschino cherries. Serve mayonnaise in small bowl placed in center of molded salad.

Mrs. Leonard Otto

AFRAID?

Afraid? Of what?
To feel the spirit's glad release?
To pass from pain to perfect peace,
The strife and strain of life to cease?
    Afraid—of that?

Afraid? Of what?
Afraid to see the Saviour's face,
To hear his welcome, and to trace
The glory gleam from wounds of grace?
    Afraid—of that?

Afraid? Of what?
A flash—a crash—a pierced heart;
Darkness—light—O heaven's art!
A wound of his a counterpart!
    Afraid? Of that?

Afraid? Of what?
To do by death what life could not—
Baptize with blood a stony plot,
Till souls shall blossom from the spot?
    Afraid? Of that?

E. H. Hamilton

❧

The greatest saint in the world is not he who prays most or fasts most; it is not he who gives most alms, or is most eminent for temperance, chastity or justice. It is he who is most thankful to God, and who has a heart always ready to praise God. This is the perfection of all virtues. Joy in God and thankfulness to God is the highest perfection of a divine and holy life.

William Law

❧

His appointment MUST be blessing
Though it MAY come in disguise;
For the end, from the beginning,
Open to His wisdom lies.

47

JELLIED COTTAGE CHEESE AND CUCUMBER SALAD (Serves 6)

1 package lemon flavored gelatine
1½ cups hot water
1½ teaspoons vinegar
¾ teaspoon salt
½ cup cooked salad dressing
¼ teaspoon paprika
4 chopped green onions, with tops
¾ cup cottage cheese
½ cup finely diced cucumber
3 tablespoons finely chopped
  green pepper

Dissolve gelatine in hot water, add vinegar, salt, salad dressing, and paprika. Beat with rotary beater to blend. Chill until slightly thickened and fold in remaining ingredients. Chill until firm. Unmold on crisp greens. Needs no dressing.

SALAD DRESSING

1½ cups water
¾ cup vinegar
2 tablespoons butter
¾ cup sugar
1 tablespoon mustard
2 tablespoons cornstarch
2 eggs
Salt

Boil water, vinegar and butter; remove from fire. Mix sugar, mustard, cornstarch, salt and beaten eggs. Add to above mixture and bring to a boil—cook until thick.
Mrs. Martin Crook

THOUSAND ISLAND DRESSING

2 cups mayonnaise
½ green pepper
½ dill pickle (or sweet)
2 tablespoons chili sauce
4 stuffed olives
1 hard boiled egg

Chop pickle, olives, pepper and egg fine. Beat chili sauce into the mayonnaise until smooth. Add the chopped ingredients and blend well.
Mrs. Oscar Green

ORANGE SALAD DRESSING

3 tablespoons flour
2 tablespoons sugar
¾ teaspoon mustard
½ teaspoon salt
1 cup orange juice
2 egg yolks beaten well
1 tablespoon butter
¼ cup lemon juice

Mix all ingredients together thoroughly. Cook in double boiler until thick. Add butter and lemon juice. Blend well. Remove from fire and chill. Use on fruit salads.
Mrs. Axel Ahlgren

PEANUT BUTTER SALAD DRESSING

1 teaspoon salt
2 tablespoons flour
1 teaspoon dry mustard
2 tablespoons sugar
Dash of cayenne
¼ cup vinegar
2 egg yolks
1 cup evaporated milk
2 tablespoons peanut butter

Blend the salt, flour, mustard, sugar, cayenne; add the egg yolks, mix well; then add the milk. Cook over boiling water until mixture thickens. Stir in the peanut butter, then the vinegar slowly. Thin with milk if too thick. Yield: 1⅛ cups.

48

"LET US GO ON"

Some of us stay at the cross,
  Some of us wait at the tomb,
Quickened and raised together with Christ,
  Yet lingering still in its gloom.
Some of us bide at the passover feast
  With Pentecost all unknown—
The triumphs of grace in the heavenly place
  That our Lord has made our own.

If the Christ who died had stopped at the cross
  His work had been incomplete,
If the Christ who was buried had stayed in the tomb
  He had only known defeat;
But the Way of the Cross never stops at the Cross,
  And the Way of the Tomb leads on
To victorious grace in the heavenly place
  Where the risen Lord has gone.

So, let us go on with the Lord
  To the fulness of God He has brought,
Unsearchable riches of glory and good
  Exceeding our uttermost thought;
Let us grow up into Christ,
  Claiming His life and its powers,—
The triumphs of grace in the heavenly place
  That our conquering Lord has made ours.

Annie Johnson Flint
Copyright, used by permission
Evangelical Publishers

BREADS

WHITE BREAD

1 cake compressed yeast
2 teaspoons sugar
2 teaspoons salt
3 quarts flour
1 quart lukewarm water or milk,
scalded and cooled
2 tablespoons melted shortening

Work the yeast and sugar together with back of spoon until they liquefy. Add them to the liquid with the salt, shortening and half the flour. Beat until smooth, then add the remainder of the flour or enough to make a dough which can be handled easily. Knead until smooth and elastic on floured breadboard. Turn smooth side uppermost in bowl, brush over lightly with melted shortening. Cover and set to rise in moderately warm place until doubled in bulk (about 3 hours). Turn onto a floured board, divide into four portions, knead a little to break up the large air bubbles, place in greased bread pans filling them half full. Cover and again allow to rise until doubled in bulk, about one hour.

Bake from ¾ to 1 hour at 375° to 400° F. for first 15 minutes, after which reduce heat for the rest of the baking. Four medium sized loaves.

Mrs. Willard Peterson

TWISTED LOAF

1 cake yeast
¼ cup lukewarm water
2 cups milk
¼ cup sugar
4 teaspoons salt
2 tablespoons shortening
2 cups water
12 cups sifted enriched flour (about)

Soften yeast in lukewarm water. Scald milk. Add sugar, salt, shortening and water. Cool to lukewarm. Add 2 cups of flour gradually, mixing it in thoroughly. Add yeast. Add remaining flour mixing well. When dough is stiff, turn out on lightly floured board and knead until smooth and satiny. Shape into smooth ball. Place in greased bowl. Cover and let rise in warm place (80° to 85° F.) until doubled in bulk. Punch down. Let rise again. When light, divide into 4 equal portions. Round up each portion into a smooth ball. Cover well and let rest 10 to 15 minutes. Mold into loaves. For twisted loaf, roll dough under hand to 2 rolls about two inches thick and longer than the length of the pan. Twist the 2 rolls around each other and place in greased bread pans. Let rise until doubled in bulk. Bake in moderately hot oven (400° to 425° F.) 40 to 45 minutes. Yield: 4 loaves.

BOSTON BROWN BREAD

½ cup corn meal
½ cup graham flour
½ cup rye flour
1 teaspoon salt
1 teaspoon soda
¼ cup molasses
1 cup sweet or sour milk

Put in well buttered cans, filling ⅔ full; put in kettle of boiling water and steam 3½ hours. This quantity will fill three one-pound baking powder cans with covers.

Mrs. T. G. Lindsay

50

MAYTIME IS SPRING CLEANING TIME

I have just been cleaning cupboards and with neat housewifely art,
I have set things all in order in the storehouse of my heart.
There are things I always meant to save and look at every day,
And then again, a lot of things I should have thrown away.

There were things in wild disorder, and mixed among the lot,
Were bitter things, and ugly ones that should have been forgot.
But there are scraps of tender dreams—a child's remembered kiss,
And a poem that my mother wrote—ah, how I treasured this.

I discovered tho', that ugly things were taking too much space
Sometimes for new and lovely ones, I couldn't find a place!
And so I've tossed the dark things out—the sullen scraps and
   tatters,
Of old-time hurts and fancied wrongs and here's what really
   matters.

Now that I've tossed the dark things out—each cringing one
   I found,
The others shine the brighter—shed a radiance all around!
My cleaning work is nearly done, and I suggest you start,
For you'll find it's mighty nice to have clean cupboards in
   your heart!

Author and source unknown

❧

The world says that men are not sinners until they have sinned.
God says that men sin because they are sinners.

❧

Not mine, but HIS must be the choice
For every passing day,
And in HIS hands I gladly leave
The keeping of my way.
Not mine—for I should make mistakes
And things would all go wrong,
But HIS—and through the darkest night
My Saviour gives a song!

SPECIAL SWEDISH RYE BREAD

1 cup water
1 cup mashed potatoes
3 cups potato water
1 tablespoon salt
½ cup molasses
1 cup dark corn syrup
2 cakes compressed yeast
7 cups sifted rye flour
1 cup whole wheat flour
1 cup soy flour

Dissolve the yeast cakes in the mixture of salt, water, mashed potato, and lukewarm potato water. Add some of the flour. Add the molasses and syrup. Mix in the flour, adding enough white flour to make a stiff dough, kneading it well. Put in a warm place to rise, then knead down again. Let rise, then form into loaves. Will make 7 loaves. Bake at 350° F. for 1 hour.

Mrs. V. E. Malmberg

ALL-BRAN PRUNE BREAD

2 cups All-Bran
⅔ cup juice from cooked prunes
⅔ cup buttermilk
½ cup sugar
1 tablespoon shortening
1 egg
1 ¼ cups flour
¼ teaspoon salt
1 ½ teaspoons soda
⅔ cup chopped cooked prunes
⅓ cup chopped nut meats

Soak All-Bran in juice drained from prunes and add buttermilk. Cream sugar and shortening thoroughly; add egg and beat well. Add All-Bran mixture. Sift flour with salt and soda and add to first mixture with prunes and nut meats. Stir only until flour disappears. Bake in a greased loaf pan in a moderate oven (325° F.) 1 hour and 20 minutes. Yield: 1 loaf. (9½ x 5½ pan.) Nut meats may be omitted.

Mrs. F. Haines

HEALTH BREAD (Raised)

1 cake fresh yeast, or 1 package granular
2 ½ cups lukewarm water, or scalded milk
½ cup brown sugar
½ cup dark molasses
½ cup lard, melted
1 teaspoon salt
2 cups graham or whole wheat flour
6 cups white flour
1 cup raisins

Soften yeast in warm water. Add brown sugar, molasses, and lard; add flour, salt, and raisins. Knead. Cover and let rise 1 hour. Knead again, cover and let rise another hour. Shape into loaves. Let rise double its bulk and bake in moderate oven (375° F.) for 1 hour. Makes three loaves.

Mrs. Wm. G. Hamstra

OATMEAL BREAD

1 cup boiling water
2 cups oatmeal, uncooked
½ cup molasses
½ teaspoon salt
1 tablespoon butter
1 cup evaporated milk
1 cake yeast, dissolved in ½ cup lukewarm water
5 cups flour

Add boiling water to oatmeal and let stand 1 hour. Add molasses, milk, salt, butter, dissolved yeast and flour. Cover and let rise until double in bulk. Knead well. Turn into greased bread pans, let rise until double in bulk and bake 15 minutes in hot oven, then 45 minutes in moderate oven. Yield: 2 loaves.

Mrs. E. F. Harder

TWISTED LOAF, See Page 50

Courtesy Wheat Flour Institute

Courtesy Wheat Flour Institute

BUTTERHORNS, See Page 56

QUICK ORANGE ROLLS, See Page 60

Courtesy Wheat Flour Institute

Courtesy Wheat Flour Institute BUTTERSCOTCH & NUT SANDWICH BREADS, See Page 54

MOTHER'S DAY

One of our modern writers, William Ross Wallace (1865) wrote:

"For the hand that rocks the cradle,
Is the hand that rules the world."

The Mother's Day Act was passed by both branches of our national Congress and approved by President Woodrow Wilson on May 8, 1914. The Bill authorized the President to issue a proclamation calling upon all government officials to display the American flag on all government buildings on the second Sunday in May. Furthermore, the President was empowered to designate this second Sunday in May as Mother's Day and to request its observance.

Proverbs 31:10-31

Who can find a virtuous woman? for her price is far above rubies.

1. She is loyal to her husband (Prov. 31:10-12).
2. She is faithful in her home (vv. 13-16).
3. She is tireless in her responsibilities (vv. 17-19).
4. She is generous toward the needy (v. 20).
5. She is fearless about circumstances (vv. 21-23).
6. She is honest in business matters (v. 24).
7. She is secured for the future (v. 25).
8. She is wise in her utterances (v. 26).
9. She is dependable in daily duties (v. 27).
10. She is praised by her children (vv. 28, 29).
11. She is beautiful in her conduct (v. 30).
12. She is appreciated by her neighbors (v. 31).

James Ostema

No language can express the power and beauty and heroism and majesty of a mother's love. It shrinks not where man cowers, and grows stronger where man faints, and over the wastes of worldly fortune sends the radiance of quenchless fidelity like a star in heaven.

POTATO BREAD

1 quart warm potato water
3 tablespoons sugar, or 4 tablespoons honey
2 tablespoons lard
2 cakes compressed yeast
3 quarts flour
2 tablespoons salt

Add the sugar to the potato water. Let cool to lukewarm and add the yeast and 4 cups flour. Mix well, add lard, 2 quarts flour and salt. Knead well until dough becomes elastic and will not stick to hands or board. Place in greased bowl and let rise until almost double in bulk. Knead again and let rise the second time, making into loaves to just half fill your pans. When raised even with top of pans place in oven. Bake 50 minutes, the first 20 minutes at 400° F. and 30 minutes at 375° F. Makes 6 loaves.

Mrs. A. J. Redard

CHRISTMAS BREAD

2 cups sifted flour
4 teaspoons baking powder
Scant ¾ cup sugar
¼ teaspoon salt
1 cup chopped candied mixed fruits
½ cup chopped nuts
2 eggs
1 cup milk
3 tablespoons butter (melted)

Sift flour, baking powder, sugar and salt. Add fruit and nuts. Beat eggs, and combine with milk and melted shortening. Add to flour mixture, stirring just enough to moisten the flour. Pour into well-greased loaf pan and let stand 30 minutes. Bake 1 hour in oven (375° F.).

Mrs. H. J. Boyd

BUTTERSCOTCH BREAD

1 egg
1 cup brown sugar
2 tablespoons melted shortening
2 cups sifted enriched flour
1 teaspoon baking powder
½ teaspoon soda
½ teaspoon salt
1 cup sour milk or buttermilk

Beat egg. Add sugar gradually, beating it in. Add shortening. Sift together flour, baking powder, soda, and salt. Add to egg mixture alternately with milk. Add chopped nuts, if desired. Pour into greased loaf pan. Bake in moderate oven (350° F.) 1 hour. Yield: 1 loaf.

NUT SANDWICH BREAD

½ cup shortening
1 cup sugar
3 eggs
2 cups sifted enriched flour
3 tablespoons baking powder
½ teaspoon salt
2 teaspoons vanilla extract
¼ cup milk
1 cup chopped nuts

Cream together shortening and sugar. Add eggs, one at a time, beating after each addition. Sift together flour, baking powder, and salt. Add flour mixture to egg mixture. Mix well. Add vanilla and milk. Add nuts and mix into smooth batter. Pour into greased loaf pan. Bake in moderate oven (350° F.) 1 hour. Yield: 1 loaf.

BANANA BREAD

1 cup sugar
½ cup shortening
2 eggs
3 mashed bananas
Pinch salt
1 teaspoon soda
½ teaspoon baking powder
1 ¾ cups flour

Mix in order given and bake in a slow oven.

Mrs. Paul Bodin

A CREED FOR MOTHERS

I believe in little children as the most precious gift of Heaven to earth.

I believe they have immortal souls created in the image of God.

I believe that in every child there are infinite possibilities for good or evil, and that the kind of influences with which we surround their early childhood largely determines their future character.

I believe in play as the child's normal effort to understand himself through free self-expression.

I believe, too, in work suitable to childhood, and that the joy in doing such work should come to the child very largely from the doing of it *well*.

I believe in wisely directing, rather than stifling activity.

I believe in inspiring the child to choose the good, the true, and the beautiful, and to contribute to the happiness of others by word and deed and gift.

I believe that in all these things my example counts for more than my precept.

I believe in cultivating the intellect and the will, but I believe, too, in soul culture, and that out of this cultivation comes the more abundant life, bringing forth the fruits of the Spirit—kindness, gentleness, joy, peace, truth, hope, faith, love, reverence for God, respect for age, consideration for each other, and thoughtfulness for all God's lowly creatures.

I believe that the calling of Motherhood is the holiest and should be the happiest of all earth's tasks.

I believe that the Christ, who was once himself a child, born of a human mother, is the one never-failing source of help for perplexed, discouraged or wearied motherhood.

Since to this work, Father, thou has called me, help me to give to it all that Thou hast given me of insight and wisdom and strength and love and gentleness and patience and forgiveness!

Intelligencer Leader

❧

'Tis sweet to place my hand in His
    Whilst all is dim;
To close my weary, aching eyes
    And follow Him.

ORANGE BREAD

2 cups all-purpose flour
1 teaspoon baking soda
¾ cup strained orange juice
¾ teaspoon salt
½ cup sugar
1 egg
2 tablespoons lemon juice
1 teaspoon grated orange rind
¼ teaspoon grated lemon rind
¼ cup shortening

Sift, then measure flour, sift again with soda, salt and sugar. Combine well-beaten egg, orange and lemon juices, grated rinds and melted shortening. Add the dry ingredients, stirring only until well mixed. Turn into a loaf pan, which has been lined with greased wax paper. Cover and let stand 20 minutes. Bake in oven (350° F.) about 1 hour. For Orange Nut Bread, add ¾ cup coarsely cut nuts to dry ingredients.

Mrs. Effie L. Willemin

DATE BREAD

1 pound dates
2 teaspoons soda
1½ cups boiling water
2¾ cups flour (sifted)
½ teaspoon baking powder
1 cup sugar
1 egg
1 tablespoon melted butter
½ teaspoon salt
½ cup nuts
1 teaspoon vanilla

Pit dates, sprinkle with soda, add boiling water. Cool. Mix dry ingredients, sift. Add egg, butter, nuts, and vanilla. Stir. Add date mixture. Stir thoroughly. Bake (375° F.) in two bread pans for 1 hour. (*Do not bake faster.*)

Mrs. Bert Wietin

STANDARD BISCUITS

2 cups flour
½ teaspoon salt
3 teaspoons baking powder
3 to 4 tablespoons shortening
¾ cup milk

Sift flour with salt and baking powder; cut in shortening until mixture resembles coarse crumbs. Add milk all at once and mix until dough follows fork around bowl. Turn out on lightly floured surface; knead gently ½ minute. Roll or pat ¾-inch thick and cut with biscuit cutter. Bake on ungreased baking sheet in hot oven (450° F.) 12 to 15 minutes. Makes 16 medium sized biscuits.

Mrs. A. J. Redard

BUTTERHORNS

1 cake compressed yeast
1 cup lukewarm water
1 cup milk
6 tablespoons sugar
1½ teaspoons salt
6 tablespoons shortening
1 egg
6 cups sifted enriched flour (about)

Soften yeast in lukewarm water. Scald milk and add sugar, salt, and shortening. When lukewarm, add 1 cup flour and beat thoroughly. Add egg, yeast, and beat well. Add enough more flour to make a soft dough. Turn out on board and knead until smooth and satiny (about 10 minutes). Place in greased bowl, cover and let rise in warm place until doubled in bulk. Knead down. Divide dough into 2 portions, cover and let rest about 15 minutes. Roll each ball of dough into circular shape about ¼-inch thick. Cut into pie-shaped pieces. Brush with melted butter or margarine and roll up, beginning at the wide end. Curve into crescents on greased baking sheet. Let rise until double in bulk. Bake in moderately hot oven (425° F.) 15 to 20 minutes. Yield: 3½ dozen small rolls.

BABY BOOK

A baby book may seem to some
    Just a trifle absurd,
"Jimmy first smiled on the 29th,"
    Or cooed his first word on the 3rd;
Or, this was the day that Cousin Mae
    Brought him that little blue hoop,
And such and such was the day, alas,
    When we thought he was getting the croup.

But then when you think of the loving hands
    That penciled each entry in,
When you think of the tender light in the eyes,
    That shone as each line would begin,
A baby book is no trifle at all,
    With its mingling of joy and of strife,
For how can a thing be a little thing,
    When it's the record of a life!

Jazbo of Old Dubuque
"In the Wake of the News"
Chicago Tribune

❧

DEVOUT MOTHERS

Sarah (Genesis 21:6)
Hannah (I Samuel 1:22)
Elizabeth (Luke 1:41)
Mary (Luke 1:46)
Eunice (II Tim. 1:5)
Honoring Mother (Exod. 20:12)
Obeying Mother (Col. 3:20)
Caring for Mother (I Tim. 5:8; John 19:25-27; Prov. 23:22)
Revering Mother's God (Exod. 20:3)

❧

Speak, Lord, in the stillness
    While I wait on Thee;
Hushed my heart to listen
    In expectancy.

QUICK ROLLS (Three-hour Process)

1 cake compressed yeast
4 tablespoons sugar
6 cups flour
1 teaspoon salt
2 cups sweet milk
4 tablespoons melted fat

Scald milk and cool; dissolve yeast and sugar in lukewarm milk; add melted fat and 1½ pints of flour sifted 3 times. Beat until perfectly smooth. Cover and let rise in a warm place for one hour. Add enough flour to make a firm dough; let rise again thirty to forty-five minutes, then make into rolls or shape into balls about the size of walnuts. Cover and let rise to top. Bake in an oven about 350° F. for twenty minutes. Remove from oven, brush top with butter, and lay a cloth over to steam.

Mrs. Fred Wassman

CHEESE DROP BISCUITS

2 cups sifted flour
½ teaspoon salt
4 tablespoons butter or other shortening
2 teaspoons baking powder
1 cup grated American cheese
1 cup milk

Sift flour once, measure, add baking powder and salt and sift again. Cut in cheese and shortening. Add milk gradually, stirring until soft dough is formed. Drop from teaspoon on ungreased baking sheet. Bake in hot oven (450° F.) 12 to 15 minutes. Makes 18. These biscuits are suitable to serve with fruit and vegetable salads for luncheon or supper.

Mrs. Titus E. Miller

SOUTHERN BUTTERMILK BISCUITS

2 cups flour
½ teaspoon soda
⅔ teaspoon salt
3 tablespoons fat
¾ cup buttermilk

Sift flour, soda and salt together. Add the fat and cut or rub it into the flour; add milk to make a soft dough; knead lightly and roll ½ inch thick. Cut out and bake in a hot oven (400°-450° F.).

Mrs. John C. Wray

DEE-LISH SCONES

2 cups sifted cake flour
2 teaspoons baking powder
½ teaspoon salt
2 teaspoons sugar
¼ cup shortening
2 eggs
⅓ cup top milk, or coffee cream

Sift flour, sugar, baking powder and salt together, and cut in the shortening. Reserve 1 egg white for a glaze; beat the rest of the eggs and add cream. Add to flour mixture, and stir until all the flour is dampened. Now stir vigorously until mixture forms a soft dough. Turn out on a slightly floured board, and knead gently for 30 seconds. Roll out ½-inch thick and cut into triangles. Place on ungreased baking sheets, brush over with slightly beaten egg white, sprinkle with sugar. Bake in oven (450° F.) 12 to 15 minutes. This makes 12 scones.

Mrs. Effie L. Willemin

MOTHERHOOD

God gives a sweet eternal gift to thee—
A little child to lead thee heavenward;
The clinging touch of fingers, satin soft,
Reaches thy heart, and lift it up to God.
God knows His gift will do the work He wills,
He clasps the child, knowing that mother hands
Will cling forever round a baby form,
And so both child and mother rest on God.
For baby's sake thou must live close to Him;
His soft eyes following thine, must see His face;
Thy lips—those lips that press his unsoiled brow,
Must for his sake be pure and undefiled;
No false or foolish word, no angry tone,
Fall on the ears God formed to hear His voice;
Thou must remember that this budding soul
Will see his God in thee, and through thee—God.
Thy hands, caressing, helping, soothing him,
Must do no Christless thing. A mother's hand
Should be the saintliest hand in God's fair earth.
A mother's feet should shine with holiness,
For small, soft, echoing steps tread after hers,
And, Oh! a mother's soul should radiant shine,
Crowned with a halo of celestial fire;
God has enriched her with the power to love,
And love should steep and soften heart and life;
A godlike love should prompt her daily rule,
Not blind to faults, but loving through them all,
And chastening, knowing that her holy Lord
Would not allow a sin to sully child of His;
Solemn the mother's work, yet very sweet,
To picture to her children—God in Christ.

Eva L. Travers

❧

*Thou art my hiding place; Thou shalt preserve me from trouble;
Thou shalt compass me about with songs of deliverance.* (Psalm 32:7)

❧

I tread no path in life to Him unknown,
I lift no burden, bear no pain alone;
My soul a calm sure hiding-place has found—
The everlasting arms my life surround.

QUICK ORANGE ROLLS

2 cups sifted enriched flour
2 tablespoons sugar
3 tablespoons baking powder
1 teaspoon salt
¼ cup shortening
1 egg
½ cup milk or orange juice
Orange sugar

Sift together flour, sugar, baking powder, and salt. Cut or rub in shortening. Beat egg, add milk or orange juice. Add all to dry ingredients. Blend with fork until dry ingredients are moistened. Turn out on lightly floured board. Knead gently for 30 seconds. Roll out into rectangular sheet ¼-inch thick. Sprinkle with Orange Sugar. Roll up jelly roll fashion and cut into 1-inch lengths. Put each slice cut side down in greased ring mold. Bake in moderately hot oven (425° F.) 15 minutes. Serve hot.
Yield: 1 ring.
ORANGE SUGAR: ½ cup sugar and grated rind of ½ orange mixed thoroughly.

COFFEE CAKE

2 cakes yeast
¼ cup lukewarm water
1 cup scalded milk
¼ cup butter
½ cup sugar
1 teaspoon salt
2 well-beaten eggs
5 cups flour

Put yeast to dissolve in ¼ cup warm water. Add sugar, butter and salt to scalded milk. Cool, then mix eggs and yeast together. Add to cooled mixture. Add 2 cups flour, beat well; then gradually add remaining flour and let stand for two hours. Divide in three parts and braid. Place on large buttered cookie sheet or pan and let stand for about an hour. Bake in 375° F. oven for approximately 30 minutes.

HONEY TOPPING:

1 tablespoon melted butter
2 tablespoons cream
1 cup confectioner's sugar
1 teaspoon vanilla extract
Walnut meats, ground or finely
    chopped

Put the topping on the cake while it is still warm.

Mrs. Norton Averill

SWEDISH TEA RING (12-inch Ring)

1 cake compressed yeast
¼ cup sugar
1 cup scalded milk
2 tablespoons butter
¾ teaspoon salt
1 egg
2½ cups flour
Butter, brown sugar, cinnamon,
    nuts, raisins

Crumble yeast into sugar and let stand until liquefied. Scald milk, add butter and salt. Cool to lukewarm and add yeast mixture and beaten egg. Stir in enough flour to make a soft dough. Turn out on lightly floured board and knead until dough is elastic and will not stick to board. Place in a greased bowl and let rise until double in bulk. Punch down and cover again. Let rise ten minutes. Then roll in rectangular sheet half an inch thick. Brush with soft butter and sprinkle with cinnamon and brown sugar. Scatter a few chopped nuts, and currants or raisins over the dough and roll up as for jelly roll. Shape into a ring on a greased baking sheet. Cut with scissors at inch intervals, almost through the ring. Turn each slice lightly on its side. Brush the ring lightly with butter and cover. Let rise until doubled. Bake at 395° F. for 25 to 30 minutes. Frost while warm with a confectioner's sugar icing and sprinkle with chopped nuts.

Miss Ella Johnson

"I CARRIED WITH ME A PICTURE"

Several years ago, five young men left their homes in West Pennsylvania and went out into the great Northwest. They found things quite different from what they were in the old home town, and the temptations were many. Some time later they had all returned to their former homes. Four of the five showed that they were much the worse because of their experiences in a strange country. But the other young man came back seemingly all the stronger and better because of the experiences through which he had passed.

When asked why he, too, had not gone the way of the other four, he calmly replied, "Because *I carried with me a picture.*" "Oh, yes, the picture of some young maiden back home, I presume?" remarked a friend. "Oh, no! Not that kind of a picture," said the young man. "It was a picture of quite a different kind. It was my last morning at home. We all sat down to breakfast as usual; father at one end of the table and my precious mother at the other. Realizing that there was to be a breaking of home ties in a few hours, conversation was not very brisk that morning. After breakfast, as was my father's custom, he took down the old Bible and started to read the morning lesson. But he didn't get very far. A lump kept coming up in his throat, and he was so blinded by tears that he could not read, and handed the book over to my mother, motioning to her to finish the reading.

"After she had finished the chapter we all knelt to pray. Father started his prayer as was his custom, but he didn't get far until that same lump came up in his throat and choked back further expression. Then mother reached over and put her hand on my shoulder and began to pray, saying, "O God we thank Thee for our son. We thank Thee for our son. We thank thee that Thou hast kept him true and faithful, and that we are able to send him out from our home chaste and clean. Keep him pure and clean and may his feet never stray from the paths of virtue, purity and the truth in which we have tried to bring him up. Bring him back to us as pure and true as he is going out from us." It was the vision of my last morning in the atmosphere of a godly home and the remembrance of my precious mother's prayer. I could not bear the thought of breaking the heart of my father and mother and dishonoring my Lord and Saviour Jesus Christ whom they taught me to love."

Oscar Lowry.

QUICK COFFEE CAKE

1 ½ cups flour
2 teaspoons baking powder
1 teaspoon salt
1 egg
1 cup sugar
¾ cup milk
4 tablespoons melted shortening
1 teaspoon vanilla

Mix and sift dry ingredients, add milk, eggs, shortening, and vanilla. Sprinkle top with cinnamon and sugar before putting in oven. Bake in moderate oven for 25 minutes.

Mrs. W. C. Florentine, Jr.

HENRICI'S COFFEE CAKE

¾ cup butter (or substitute)
1 ½ cups sugar
Pinch of salt
3 teaspoons baking powder
1 cup milk
3 eggs, beaten one at a time
2 tablespoons lemon juice
Grated rind of lemon
3 cups cake flour

Grease pan well, and sprinkle bottom of pan with pecans. Bake in moderate oven 1 hour. Use tube pan. When done, turn upside down and sprinkle with powdered sugar.

HONEY TWIST

1 cup milk, scalded
½ cup sugar
¼ cup lukewarm water
¼ cup butter
1 teaspoon salt
2 eggs
2 cakes yeast
5 to 6 cups flour

TOPPING:

¼ cup butter
⅔ cup confectioner's sugar
1 egg white
2 tablespoons honey, warmed

Pour the hot milk over butter, sugar and salt. Crumble the yeast into the lukewarm water to soften. Cool the milk mixture to lukewarm, add the yeast and the well-beaten eggs. Beat in the 5 cups flour to make a soft dough (add more flour if needed), then turn out on a floured board and knead until dough is smooth. Form into a ball and place in a greased bowl. Cover and let rise until double in bulk. When light, shape into a long roll about 1 inch in diameter. Coil the roll into a greased cake pan, begin at outside edge, and cover bottom of pan. Brush with Honey Topping, let rise until double in bulk, bake in 375° F. oven 25 to 30 minutes.

Mrs. Effie Willemin

COFFEE CAKE

1 cake yeast
1 ¼ cups scalded milk
5 cups flour
¼ cup sugar
1 ½ cups raisins, seeded
¼ cup butter
2 eggs, beaten
1 teaspoon salt
Rind of ½ lemon

Dissolve yeast in scalded milk that has been cooled to lukewarm; add 1½ cups flour and mix until smooth; let stand until light and puffy. Add eggs, sugar, raisins, salt, remaining flour, and lemon rind. Mix to a stiff dough and knead thoroughly. Let stand until double in bulk. Divide into 2 equal parts, cut each into 3 uniform parts, then roll each part like a candy stick. Braid very loosely. Put on a large cookie sheet and cover, let rise until light, then bake for 25 minutes in a 325° F. oven, or until nice and brown. When cool, ice by mixing a few drops of hot water with powdered sugar and vanilla, and sprinkle a few chopped nuts over the top.

MOTHER TO SON

Do you know that your soul is of my soul such part
That you seem to be fiber and core of my heart?
None other can pain me as you, dear, can do;
None other can please me, or praise me, as you.

Remember, the world is quick with its blame,
If shadows or stain ever darken your name.
"Like mother, like son," is a saying so true—
The world will judge largely of mother by you.

Be yours then, the task—if task it shall be—
To force the proud world to do homage to me,
Be sure it will say, when its verdict you've won:
"She reaped as she sowed: lo, this is her son."

Author and source unknown

~~~

A busy mother was one day regretting that she could do so little church work and take so small a part in Christian enterprises. "I shall have only a life of housework to show at last," she said rather sadly to a friend one day. "Why, mother," exclaimed her little daughter, who overhead the words, "all we children will stand up and tell all you've done for us—everything! I shouldn't s-pose they'd want anything better than *good mothers* up in heaven." And the friend answered: "The child is right. Earth will send to heaven no better saints than the true Christian mothers who have done their best."

The Home Messenger

~~~

Keep me, Lord, for darkness gathers
Round about the path I tread;
Keep me, Lord, and let my footsteps
Ever by Thy Word be led.

SOUR MILK DOUGHNUTS

2 eggs
1 cup sugar
¼ cup melted shortening
1 teaspoon vanilla or ¼ teaspoon
  nutmeg
1 cup sour milk or buttermilk
4 cups general purpose flour
4 teaspoons baking powder
¼ teaspoon soda
¾ teaspoon salt

Beat the eggs until light, add the sugar, and beat until smooth. Stir in the melted shortening and the vanilla or nutmeg. Add alternately the milk and the flour (sifted with the baking powder, soda, and salt), mixing to a smooth, soft dough. Turn out on a floured surface, knead lightly, and pat or roll ½-inch thick. Cut with a floured doughnut cutter, and fry in deep, hot fat (375° F.) until golden brown, turning once. Drain on absorbent paper and serve plain or dredged in sugar. (A little ground clove added to the sugar gives an enticing flavor.) This makes about 30 doughnuts.

Mrs. Norman M. Karsten

RAISED DOUGHNUTS

2 cakes compressed yeast
¼ cup lukewarm water
1½ teaspoons corn syrup
½ cup scalded milk
½ cup shortening
2 teaspoons salt
¾ cup corn syrup
5 cups sifted all-purpose flour

Crumble yeast into a small bowl; add lukewarm water and 1½ teaspoons corn syrup. Set in a warm place until it becomes light and spongy (about 15 minutes). Pour scalded milk over shortening and stir until melted. Add salt, ¾ cup corn syrup, and mix. Cool until lukewarm. Add yeast mixture and blend; add eggs and mix well; add flour and knead to a smooth dough. Cover and let rise until double in bulk (about 2 hours). Roll dough ½-inch thick and cut with 2½-inch doughnut cutter. Place on greased pan 1 inch apart. Cover and let rise in warm place until very light. Fry in hot grease (360° F.) about 1½ inches deep until brown, turning once. Drain on absorbent paper. Makes 2½ dozen. Sprinkle lightly with sugar if desired.

Mrs. Emerald Jones

FRENCH DOUGHNUTS

1 cup sifted flour
1 cup milk
1 heaping teaspoon butter
1 pinch salt
2 heaping teaspoons baking
  powder
3 eggs
1 teaspoon vanilla

Sift flour and baking powder. Heat milk with butter in it to boiling point. Then add flour and mix well. Cool, then add eggs one at a time. Bake like doughnuts in hot lard.

Mrs. Roy Johnson

"FET BALLEN" FRITTERS (Holland Recipe)

1 cup sugar
1 egg
2 teaspoons melted shortening
1½ cups milk
1 quart flour
1 cup currants or raisins
1 apple (sliced fine)
2 teaspoons baking powder

Stir the mixture well and drop by spoonfuls in hot shortening as for doughnuts.

Mrs. H. Nauta

IF GOD FORGOT

If God forgot the world for just one day,
Then little children would not laugh and play;
Birds would not in the woodlands sing,
And roses would not beautify the spring.
No gentle showers throughout the summer long,
No autumn fields to cheer the heart with song,
No rising sun, no moon to give its light,
No placid lake reflect the stars of night.
No friend to help us on the toilsome road,
No one to help us bear the heavy load.
No light to shine upon the pilgrim way,
No one to care, or wipe the tear away.
No listening ear to hear the lost one call,
No eye to see the righteous battler fall.
No balm of Gilead to dull the throbbing pain,
No one to comfort and the heart sustain.
Millions would die in unforgiven sin,
With none to bring the lost and straying in;
Yea, this great universe would melt away,
If God forgot the world for just one day.

J. G. W. Kirschner

❧

Note that while God loved the whole world, it is the saints who are called the "beloved of God." They are His household, His dear children. Sinners should believe that God loved them and gave His Son for them; but saints, that they are the "beloved of God." The unsaved are never named God's "beloved." A man, even, may, and should, love his neighbor: but his wife and children are "his beloved."

William R. Newell

❧

Adoringly we wonder,
As grace proclaims that we
To Thee, our Lord, united
Are ever one with Thee.
And when in heaven's glory
Most gladly we awake,
We'll wear Thy very likeness,
And of Thy joys partake.

CAKES

VICTORY CAKE WITH SEVEN VARIATIONS

2 cups sifted all-purpose flour
1 level tablespoon baking powder
½ teaspoon salt
⅔ cup shortening
¾ cup beet sugar
1 teaspoon vanilla extract
2 eggs, well beaten
⅔ cup milk

Mix and sift together flour, baking powder and salt. Cream sugar and shortening until fluffy as whipped cream. (If hard shortening is used, cream thoroughly before adding sugar. Vegetable shortenings come already creamed and should be kept at room temperature at all times.) Add vanilla extract. Stir in the well-beaten eggs. Add sifted flour mixture alternately with milk, starting and finishing with flour. Blend thoroughly between each addition, working quickly and lightly to keep the batter as smooth and fluffy as possible. Bake in a prepared loaf pan, 9x5x3 inches, in a moderate oven (350° F.) for about 50 minutes. An 8-inch square pan 2 inches deep will require about the same time. Or bake in two prepared 9-inch layer cake pans at 375° F. for about 25 or 30 minutes.

VICTORY CAKE VARIATIONS

1. Nut Loaf Cake
Add ½ teaspoon cinnamon to the flour mixture before sifting. Add ½ to 1 cup chopped nuts to the finished batter.

2. Peanut Brittle Cake
Use only ½ cup sugar instead of ¾ cup. Add 1 cup crushed peanut brittle to the finished batter.

3. Chocolate Marble Cake
Divide batter in half. Melt 1 square (1 ounce) unsweetened chocolate over hot water; add to one-half of batter. Drop batters by alternate tablespoons into a greased, paper-lined loaf pan.

4. Chocolate Spice Cake
Add ½ teaspoon cloves and ½ teaspoon cinnamon to flour before sifting. Add ¼ teaspoon grated orange rind to creamed sugar and shortening. Melt 2 squares (2 ounces) unsweetened chocolate over hot water. Add to creamed mixture.

5. Chocolate Chip Cake
Fold 4 ounces semi-sweet chocolate, coarsely grated, into finished batter.

6. Spicy Raisin Cake
Add ½ teaspoon each of cloves, cinnamon and allspice to flour mixture before sifting. Add 1 cup chopped seeded raisins to flour and spice mixture after sifting. Fold into creamed mixture alternately with milk in the usual way.

7. Mocha Nut Cake
Substitute ⅔ cup strong cold coffee for milk. Add ⅔ cup chopped nuts to the finished batter.

U. S. Beet Sugar Association

HONEY AND WAFFLES

Did you ever notice God's menu for the children of Israel on their journey through the wilderness? "Honey and waffles for breakfast, and quail on toast for supper."

After their wonderful deliverance at the Red Sea, one would suppose that the people would never murmur again. But hardly were they through singing their song of deliverance before they began to complain of their privations, and long for the flesh pots of Egypt.

What was God's answer? Honey and waffles for breakfast, and quail broiled, fried, or fricasseed for dinner. The manna was round and white like waffles, and had the taste of honey. Ex. 16:13,31.

This story illumines like a searchlight the duty of daily Bible reading, for while the manna answered their objections, and assured them of God's protection and care, it was also to be a test of their obedience.

1. It must be gathered freshly each day. It would not keep until morning, much less could one gather a week's supply on a single day. Neither will half a dozen chapters read on Sunday suffice for our spiritual needs all the week.

2. Each person must gather the manna for himself. No foraging squad could gather for the whole tribe, any more than the pastors of a city can gather the spiritual food needed by their congregation. There is a blessing in the gathering which the individual cannot afford to miss.

3. The manna was suited to the needs of all. The strong and the weak, the aged and the young, found it alike suited to their tastes and needs. John Ruskin says: "*Study* the Bible; make it your first daily business to understand some portion of it, and make it your business the rest of the day to obey what you understand." He pays the highest tribute to his mother for having required him to commit to memory some of the most sublime and practical passages of the Bible, and then gives a list of those chapters with which, he says, "she established my soul in life."

4. And this manna and quail diet was furnished by God during all the forty years of their wandering in the wilderness. No wonder they called it "Bread from Heaven" and "Angel's Food,"—for so it was.

5. One significant fact of their supernatural food was this, that when they came to measure what they had gathered and compare

67

BUTTERCUP CAKE

½ cup shortening, part butter
1 ½ cups sugar
2 eggs
2 ¼ cups flour
1 cup buttermilk
½ teaspoon soda
½ teaspoon baking powder
½ teaspoon salt
1 teaspoon vanilla
¼ teaspoon almond
¼ teaspoon lemon
¼ teaspoon orange

Cream the shortening, add the sugar and cream well. Add the well-beaten eggs. Sift the flour with the dry ingredients—with the exception of the soda which is dissolved in the buttermilk—and add alternately with the buttermilk. Add the flavoring. If made in layers, bake 30 to 35 minutes at 350° F.; if a square cake, bake it 45 to 50 minutes. Frost with white icing (same flavoring as cake). Decorate the edge with grated orange or lemon rind to resemble a border of flowers. Syrup may be substituted for sugar in this proportion: ½ cup sugar, 1 cup white corn syrup, ¾ cup milk.

Mrs. G. M. Reed

LAZY DAISY CAKE

2 eggs
1 cup sugar
½ cup boiling milk
1 tablespoon butter
¼ teaspoon salt
1 cup flour
1 teaspoon baking powder
1 teaspoon vanilla, or other
   flavoring

Beat eggs well, add sugar slowly and mix thoroughly. Melt butter in boiling milk and add to the above mixture, stirring constantly. Sift dry ingredients 3 times and add to batter. Add vanilla. Bake in square baking dish or paper muffin cups for 30 minutes in 350° F. oven. The cake may be varied by adding ½ cup chopped nuts to the batter. The cake may be served plain, or covered with fresh or canned fruit, or a soft custard sauce, powdered sugar or any frosting desired. It is also delicious served with a dab of whipped cream topped with a maraschino cherry.

Mrs. Albert Coleman

SUBSTITUTE CAKE

2 cups flour, unbleached
2 cups bran (fresh)
¾ teaspoon salt
¾ cup buttermilk
1 ½ cups sugar
3 tablespoons melted butter
2 teaspoons baking powder
1 package seedless raisins
2 eggs
¾ teaspoon baking soda

Put soda in cup of buttermilk. Mix dry ingredients, sifted together. Beat the eggs, then add buttermilk, melted butter, and the raisins that have been floured. Bake in 350° F. oven about 65 minutes in a greased large bread pan lined with wax paper.

Mrs. G. C. Hughes

POOR MAN'S CAKE

1 cup brown sugar
1 cup hot water
1 cup raisins
1 heaping tablespoon lard
1 teaspoon cinnamon
½ teaspoon nutmeg
2 cups flour
½ teaspoon baking powder
½ teaspoon salt
½ teaspoon baking soda
1 teaspoon vanilla

Boil the ingredients—sugar, water, raisins, lard, cinnamon and nutmeg—five minutes. Cool. Add sifted flour, baking powder, and salt. Then add the baking soda which has been mixed in a little cold water. Add the flavoring. Bake 1 hour in a slow oven (250°-325° F.).

Mrs. Fred Oldfield

PINEAPPLE UPSIDE-DOWN CAKE, See Page 72

Courtesy Bowman Dairy Co.

Courtesy The Quaker Oats Co.

SPECIAL HOLIDAY CAKE, See Page 76 ➡

COTTAGE CHEESE TORTE, See Page 74

Courtesy Bowman Dairy Co.

Courtesy Bowman Dairy Co.

BURNT SUGAR CAKE, See Page 74

it with the amount which Moses had directed, the most eager and industrious had nothing over, and the most feeble had no lack.

This was certainly miraculous. But no more so than the way in which God illumines the Word and applies it to *our* daily needs. The other morning I read Ps. 122:6, "Pray for the peace of Jerusalem: they shall prosper that love thee." I have read that verse scores of times, but never has it gripped me so strongly, rebuked me so sharply, or evoked so much prayer for *God's chosen people*.

For devotional uses the *Psalms* are perhaps the best, because they cover so wide a range of experience. In the morning read Ps. 19, and at evening, Ps. 8. If you are going on a journey, Ps. 121 is appropriate.

The *Gospels* also are excellent for devotional reading because there we come in contact with the words and works of Jesus. We see how He lived in the home and by the wayside, in the carpenter's shop, and by the open grave. We see Him in public life and in private ministry, always the same, never hurried, never worried, always thinking of *others* and never of Himself. We see Him playing with the *children*, watching the hens in the dooryard, and the birds on the trees, the growing grain and fading flowers. In *everything* He saw *God's* love and care, and from all things natural He drew some spiritual lesson for His own or another's comfort.

If it be asked how much one should read at a time for devotional purposes, I answer; read until your heart burns. You may read a chapter or a book or a single verse, but read, if you can, until you are consciously in touch with God, and then with the Father's morning kiss upon your lips, you are ready to meet the outside world.

It is a good plan when one has read a chapter to ask himself—
1. What is the subject of this chapter?
2. Is there any example in it for *me* to follow?
3. Any error for me to avoid?
4. Any duty for me to perform?
5. Any promise for me to claim?
6. Any prayer for me to offer?

And remember that one verse of Scripture committed to memory, and really *believed* or *obeyed*, is worth more than a whole book read hastily and without thought.

Howard W. Pope

BUTTERMILK CAKE

1 cup butter
2 cups sugar
1 cup buttermilk
3 cups pastry flour
1 teaspoon soda
1 teaspoon cream of tartar
½ teaspoon salt
1 teaspoon vanilla
6 egg whites

Cream the butter. Add sugar gradually, creaming continually. Add alternately the buttermilk and sifted dry ingredients. Add the flavoring, and fold in stiffly beaten egg whites. Bake in a 9x13-inch pan in 350° F. oven for 40 minutes, or until done.

Mrs. Louise Hill

DEVILS FOOD CAKE

½ cup butter
1 ¼ cups sugar
2 eggs
1 ¾ cups flour
1 teaspoon salt
1 teaspoon soda
1 cup milk
2 squares melted chocolate
1 teaspoon vanilla

Combine the ingredients in the order given. Bake in a moderate oven.

Mrs. John Holland

CHOCOLATE ANGEL FOOD CAKE

1 ½ cups egg whites
2 cups sugar
½ cup cocoa
1 cup bread flour
1 teaspoon cream of tartar
¼ teaspoon salt
1 teaspoon vanilla

Sift the cocoa and sugar together with ½ teaspoon cream of tartar, 4 times. Whip the whites of eggs until stiff. Add the salt and the rest of the cream of tartar. Add the sugar and cocoa, then the sifted flour folded in. Put in angel food tin and place in cold oven; set the thermometer on 300° F. and start the oven. Bake for 50 minutes or until done. Turn upside down and put wet cloth around tin, and cover with a dry one. Let set for 1 hour, or until cold.

CHOCOLATE COATING:

2 squares unsweetened chocolate
1 cup sifted confectioner's sugar
2 tablespoons water
1 egg
1 tablespoon butter

Combine the chocolate, sugar and water in the top of a double boiler. Cook over boiling water 8 minutes, stirring frequently. Remove from the boiling water and add 1 well-beaten egg, beating thoroughly; beat in 1 tablespoon butter.

Mrs. Louise Hill

QUICK COCOA CAKE

6 tablespoons cocoa
2 cups flour
1 ½ cups sugar
1 teaspoon baking soda
⅛ teaspoon salt
2 eggs
¾ cup butter, melted
1 cup cold water

Sift first 5 ingredients into the mixing bowl. Add the rest, but do not stir until all ingredients are in. Then beat well. Bake in 2 layers, in moderate oven (350° F.) for 40 minutes. Frost with chocolate frosting.

Mrs. J. W. Tenjack

UPON GRADUATION

With eyes that look along the road of years

    Far stretching into devious length ahead,

You stand today, beset with hopes and fears

    Not knowing what, as on your steps are led,

The years hold for you; what of joy or care

    Awaits you on the road as yet untrod.

But still with strength of youth art standing there

    Trusting thy future to the hand of God.

Be strong, O Youth, and strive as forth you go,

    To fight for truth; be bold in her defense.

Uphold the right and on her cause bestow

    Thy strength, nor give a thought to recompense.

Search out the plan thy God hath made for you

    And know thy life will then be great and true.

Edith Dunn Bolar
Moody Monthly

♁

In all thy ways acknowledge him, and he shall direct thy paths.
(Prov. 3:6)

*Have not I commanded thee? Be strong and of a good courage; be
not afraid, neither be thou dismayed: for the Lord thy God is with
thee whithersoever thou goest.* (Joshua 1:9)

. . . . *I being in the way, the Lord led me.* (Gen. 24:27)

♁

God is light! His way is perfect,

    Seeing not with human sight,

Choosing not with human wisdom,

    He is doing only right;

Oh, remember, in thy blindness,

    God Himself is always Light.

HONEY CHOCOLATE CAKE

2 ½ cups cake flour
1 teaspoon baking powder
¾ teaspoon soda
1 teaspoon vanilla
¾ cup honey or syrup
¾ cup brown sugar
½ cup shortening
½ cup cocoa
2 eggs
1 ¼ cups sour milk
½ teaspoon salt

Cream honey, sugar and shortening. Add cocoa and stir well. Add eggs one at a time and stir vigorously. Add sour milk and sifted dry ingredients and stir lightly. Add vanilla. Makes three 9-inch layers.

Mrs. Willis Griffin

PINEAPPLE UPSIDE-DOWN CAKE

CARAMEL MIXTURE FOR BOTTOM OF CAKE PAN:

¼ cup butter
1 can sliced pineapple (five slices)
1 cup light brown sugar
5 maraschino cherries

BATTER:

¼ cup butter
¾ cup sugar
1 egg
1 teaspoon vanilla
¼ teaspoon salt
1 ½ cups pastry flour (sifted)
2 teaspoons baking powder
½ cup milk

Spread butter in bottom of a nine-inch cake pan and add brown sugar. Drain pineapple and place slices on top of the sugar. In the center of each pineapple slice, place a maraschino cherry. Cover this with batter made according to the following recipe, and bake the cake in a moderate oven at 350° F. for forty-five minutes. Remove cake from pan immediately after taking from oven.

Cream butter and sugar. Add the unbeaten egg and the flavoring and beat well. Measure the dry ingredients. Sift together the flour, baking powder and salt. Add dry ingredients to the creamed mixture alternately with the milk.

HOT MILK SPONGE CAKE

2 eggs
1 cup sugar
1 cup cake flour
1 teaspoon baking powder
½ teaspoon salt
½ cup milk
1 heaping tablespoon shortening

Beat the whole eggs with electric or hand rotary beater until double in bulk. Gradually add the sugar, beating until all is used. Heat the milk and shortening almost to a boil while sifting flour. Sift flour and measure 1 cup. Sift again with baking powder and salt. Fold into egg and sugar mixture. Fold in hot milk and shortening a little at a time. Put in an 8x8x2-inch square tin (grease bottom but not sides). Bake in 350° F. oven for about ½ hour.

WHITE SYRUP FROSTING:

½ cup white syrup
1 egg white

Heat the white syrup almost to a boil. Beat 1 egg white till stiff. Gradually pour in the hot syrup, beating all the while. Continue beating till it holds its shape. It becomes the consistency of marshmallows and holds up well for days. Honey may be substituted for white syrup.

Mrs. F. Lardie

TRINITY

She was so small so short a time ago
   She lay against my heart, a baby thing,
And now I watch the lovely flush and glow
   Illumine her that only love can bring.

They told me I should feel hot, jealous pain
   When first she turned to other arms from mine;
I have not found it so. Not loss, but gain
   It is for me, she's found a thing so fine.

I love him with a strange and tender love—
   This tall, sweet boy, whose laughing, clear, young eyes,
Saw dreams come true in her, and sought to prove
   Her not a child, but woman, woman wise.

They love absorbed. I see her wholly his
   As he is hers until the end of time.
And yet,—yet, I know that each one is
   In some way wholly, deeply, sweetly mine.

Author and source unknown

༺✦༻

DAUGHTER-IN-LAW

There are no words that I am master of
   With which to thank you, God, for my son's wife;
This girl who is part mother in her love,
   Part young girl, and part woman, and her life
So gathered up in flame to meet the one
     Who is my son.
I yield him to her, I who have so long
   Been lovingly preparing him for her.
I would not bind them with one selfish thong
   That through its constant chafing might deter
Their love upon the high road, they must be
   Free as the wind is free,
Dear God, I am so grateful that my son
   In searching for a woman found this one.

Grace Noll Crowell
The Lifted Lamp
Harper and Brothers

APPLESAUCE FRUIT CAKE

        3 cups hot applesauce
        1 cup butter
        2 cups sugar
        4 teaspoons soda
    4 ½ cups flour
        1 teaspoon nutmeg
        1 teaspoon cloves
        1 teaspoon salt
    2 ½ teaspoons cinnamon
        1 pound seeded raisins
        1 box currants
        1 pound dates
        ½ pound citron
        ½ pound candied orange
        ½ pound lemon
        ½ pound pineapple
        ½ pound cherries
        ½ pound walnuts

Put the hot applesauce through a colander. Add the butter and sugar, and let stand overnight. Next morning, add the remaining ingredients. Bake in a slow oven 2½ to 3 hours. It makes 2 loaves. I have baked them in 1 pound loaves, making about 8 pounds of cake.

Mrs. John Holland

COTTAGE CHEESE TORTE (Serves 12)

        1 package zwieback
    1 ½ cups sugar
        1 teaspoon cinnamon
        ¼ pound butter (melted)
        2 jars cottage cheese
        4 eggs
    3 ½ tablespoons flour
        1 teaspoon salt
        1 teaspoon vanilla
        ½ cup cream

Roll zwieback to fine crumbs and mix with one-half cup of the sugar, the cinnamon and the melted butter. Reserve one cup of the mixture for top of cake. Line sides and bottom of cake pan with remaining mixture.

Force the cottage cheese through a ricer or sieve. Beat eggs well and add to cheese. Mix remaining one cup of sugar, the flour, salt, vanilla and the cream. Add to egg-cheese mixture. Pour filling into lined pan. Cover with remaining crumb mixture. Bake in a 300° F. oven for approximately one hour. Turn off heat and leave cheese cake in oven one hour longer.

BURNT SUGAR CAKE

        ½ cup butter
        1 cup sugar
        3 eggs (separated)
        ½ cup milk
        ½ cup burnt sugar mixture
    1 ½ cups cake flour (sifted)
        2 teaspoons baking powder
        ½ teaspoon salt

Prepare burnt sugar as follows: Brown one-half cup sugar in skillet, stirring constantly. Add one-half cup hot water and heat until all of the caramelized sugar is dissolved. Cool.

The cake:

Cream butter thoroughly. Add sugar gradually, creaming mixture until light after each addition. Beat egg yolks and add to butter-sugar mixture.

Sift together the flour, baking powder and salt and add to creamed mixture alternately with the milk and burnt sugar mixture. Finally fold in the stiffly beaten egg whites. Bake in two layer pans in a moderate oven (350° F.), for about one-half hour. Top with Seven Minute or Boiled Frosting.

A MESSAGE TO THE BRIDE AND GROOM

As at the marriage altar now you stand,
Dear ones, united in love's holy bond,
The Saviour reaches forth his nail-pierced hand,
And bids thee walk with Him the path beyond.

He offers thy unfailing guide to be
Along life's devious and uncertain way,—
To every worth-while joy He holds the key,
Joys He would have thee know from day to day.

Within thy doors He ever would abide,
The blessing of His presence to impart,
To be thy counsellor whate'er betide,
For thou art precious to His loving heart.

Grant at thy table unto Him a place,—
Yea, yield to Him the headship of thy home;
Let all thy plans be guided by His grace,
And all thy wishes centered in His own.

Let His blest Word be thy unfailing light,
His promises thy bulwark day by day,
His pow'r thy ceaseless source of strength and might,
His love thy sunshine all along life's way.

So shall the future hold, dear ones, for thee
Joy which no storm or stress can ever sway;
Peace from Above, abundant, full and free,
And glory that shall never pass away.

Blest is the home on Christ, the Saviour, built,—
Sweet foretaste of that Home beyond the sky,
Where through the precious blood on Calv'ry spilt,
All the redeemed shall enter bye and bye.

Avis B. Christiansen

TULLARD (Dutch White Fruit Cake)

1 cup granulated sugar
½ cup shortening
2 eggs, well beaten
1 cup milk
2 cups sifted flour
2 teaspoons baking powder
1 cup currants or small raisins
¼ pound citron
Grated rind and juice of 1 orange
2 ounces chopped walnuts
1 teaspoon vanilla

Mix fruit well with a small amount of flour and ½ teaspoon baking powder, before adding to batter. Bake in tube pan in slow oven as any fruit cake.

Mrs. H. Nauta

GOLDEN FRUIT CAKE

1 pound candied fruit
1 cup white raisins
1 cup almonds, cut
2 cups all-purpose flour
1 teaspoon baking powder
¼ teaspoon salt
1 cup sugar
½ cup butter
3 eggs, unbeaten
1 teaspoon vanilla
¼ teaspoon almond extract
½ cup orange juice, or any light
   fruit juice

Combine fruit and nuts with flour after it has been sifted with baking powder and salt. Cream sugar and butter until light and fluffy. Then add one egg at a time, beating well after each. Add flavoring, fruit and flour mixture to the above, and fruit juice last of all. Place two layers of heavy brown paper in bottom of pan and grease well. Bake about 2 hours in a large loaf pan or casserole in a 300° F. oven. Also put a pan of water on the floor of the oven during baking.

Mrs. Herbert Raedeke

SPECIAL HOLIDAY CAKE

2 cups flour
1 cup chopped nuts
1 cup raisins
⅓ cup chopped citron (if desired)
½ teaspoon soda
1 teaspoon baking powder
½ teaspoon salt
1 teaspoon cinnamon
1 teaspoon allspice
½ teaspoon nutmeg
½ cup shortening (part butter)
1 cup brown sugar, firmly packed
2 eggs, well beaten
¾ cup sour milk or buttermilk
1 teaspoon vanilla

BUTTERSCOTCH FROSTING:

1¼ cups brown sugar (firmly
   packed)
1¼ cups granulated sugar
1¼ cups milk
2 tablespoons butter

Sift flour once, measure. Mix ¼ cup with nuts, raisins and citron. Sift remainder of flour with soda, baking powder, salt, cinnamon, allspice and nutmeg. Cream shortening until soft, add sugar gradually and cream until light and fluffy. Stir in well-beaten eggs. Add flour mixture alternately with milk, beating well after each addition. Stir in vanilla. Add floured nuts and fruits and stir until well distributed throughout the batter. Turn into a greased 8-inch tube pan or greased 8-inch square pan and bake in a moderate oven (350° F.) for 45 to 50 minutes or until a toothpick inserted in the center comes out clean. Remove from oven and let stand about 15 minutes. Remove from pan and cool on cake rack. Frost with Butterscotch Frosting and garnish with thin strips of citron and red cinnamon candies, if desired.

Combine sugars and milk, bring to a boil while stirring constantly. Then cook without stirring to 232° F., or until a small amount of the syrup will form a soft ball when dropped in cold water. Cool to lukewarm (100° F.). Add butter. Beat until creamy, then spread on cake.

PRAYER OF A YOUNG WIFE

Dear Father, hear my prayer tonight,
And teach Thy child to be
The woman that my husband's love
Already sees in me.

He calls me good, and gentle, Lord.
Oh, may he never find
That I am less than what he thinks!
Lord, help me to be kind.

I must have faith to meet his doubt,
And strength when he is weak,
I would learn peace for every storm,
And wisdom when I speak.

Lord, help me always to maintain
The standards of his creed,
And give me courage, strength and love
To answer constant need.

Dear Father! Hear me as I pray,
And ever guide us in Thy way.

Clara Bernhardt

❧

WEDDING ANNIVERSARIES

First Year, Paper
Second Year, Cotton
Third Year, Linen
Fourth Year, Silk
Fifth Year, Wood
Sixth Year, Iron
Seventh Year, Copper
Eighth Year, Bronze
Ninth Year, Pottery
Tenth Year, Tin

Fifteenth Year, Crystal
Twentieth Year, China
Twenty-Fifth Year, Silver
Thirtieth Year, Pearl
Thirty-fifth Year, Coral
Fortieth Year, Ruby
Forty-fifth Year, Sapphire
Fiftieth Year, Gold
Fifty-fifth Year, Emerald
Seventy-Fifth Year, Diamond

READY FROSTED SPICE CAKE

¼ cup shortening
¾ cup firmly packed brown sugar
1 egg (well beaten)
1 teaspoon baking powder
½ teaspoon soda
½ teaspoon cinnamon
¼ teaspoon cloves
¼ teaspoon salt
1 ⅜ cups flour, sifted once before
    measuring
¼ cup chopped dates
½ cup sour milk or buttermilk

FROSTING:

2 egg whites
1 cup brown sugar
¼ cup chopped nuts
¼ teaspoon salt
¼ teaspoon vanilla

Cream shortening until it is light, gradually add the brown sugar, continuing to cream until the mixture is spongy. Then beat in the well-beaten egg. Sift dry ingredients together several times, and mix in chopped dates. Add the dry ingredients to the creamed mixture alternately with sour milk or buttermilk.

Whip egg whites until stiff. Add salt. Gradually add sugar. Beat well. Lastly, add vanilla and chopped nuts. Spread lightly over the top of cake batter. Bake in a moderately hot oven (375° F.) for about 35 to 40 minutes; until an inserted tester comes out clean.

DATE AND APPLESAUCE CAKE

½ cup butter
1 cup light brown sugar
2 eggs
1 ½ cups applesauce
2 teaspoons soda
2 cups flour
½ teaspoon cinnamon
½ teaspoon nutmeg
¼ teaspoon cloves
1 cup chopped dates
1 cup nut meats
1 teaspoon vanilla
1 cup seedless raisins

Cream butter, add sugar. Cream well and add eggs. Stir soda into applesauce. Mix dates, nuts, raisins and flour together, which has been sifted with the spices. Combine all ingredients and turn onto a greased and floured tube or loaf pan. Bake in a slow oven for 1 hour or longer. If you choose, ice with a plain butter icing.

Mrs. A. J. Redard

APPLE STRUDEL

2 cups flour
3 teaspoons baking powder
½ teaspoon salt
3 tablespoons sugar
¼ cup shortening
⅔ to ¾ cup milk
1 teaspoon cinnamon
½ cup sugar
¾ cup chopped apples

ICING:

1 tablespoon top milk
Confectioner's sugar, to make a
    paste
Vanilla

Sift flour and measure 2 cups, sift the 2 cups with the baking powder, salt and sugar. Cut shortening into the dry ingredients until evenly distributed, add milk to make a soft dough. Turn this onto a lightly floured board and knead gently. Roll dough into a rectangular shape ¼-inch thick, brush melted butter over the top. Now add the cinnamon, sugar and chopped apple which have been mixed, and cover the dough. Then roll it in jelly roll fashion to enclose the fruit filling. Place on a greased baking sheet, shaping dough in the form of a semicircle. Bake in a hot oven (400° F.) for 30 minutes. Sprinkle brown sugar over the top during the last 15 minutes of baking—or the baked strudel may be frosted with a thin icing—and sprinkled with chopped nuts. Orange juice or pineapple juice may be used instead of milk.

Mrs. Effie Willemin

10th

Ten years together. Can it be
A whole decade has gone
Since you pledged to eternity
The love that made you one?
Ten years indeed! And blest has been
The way o'er which you've trod:
And, oh, what wonders you have seen,
Wrought by the hand of God.
And though your love was sweet the day
When first you pledged your troth,
It has grown sweeter all the way,
More precious to you both.
New heights and depths of Love Divine
Have blended with your own,
Filling your inmost souls with joy
Before to you unknown.

Avis B. Christiansen

25th

A quarter of a century you've walked life's way together,
Through joy and sorrow, loss and gain, and through
    all kinds of weather;
And as you've shared its pain and grief, as well as
    many a blessing,
You've found your gladness more complete, your sadness
    less distressing.
For love can tinge the darkest cloud with glints of
    heavenly sweetness,
And add to e'en our deepest joys a sense of rich
    completeness.
So on this silver wedding day life holds a fuller
    meaning
Than e'er it did in by-gone hours of wishful, empty
    dreaming.
Your Father's hand hath never failed in any time of trial,
And never when His help you've sought have you met
    stern denial.
Today with hearts still undismayed, you face the
    unknown morrow,
Strong in His might, and unafraid of turmoil, pain
    or sorrow.

Avis B. Christiansen

JELLY ROLL

5 eggs
1 cup sugar
2 tablespoons lemon juice
1 cup cake flour sifted

Beat yolks of eggs, add the sugar gradually. Add lemon juice, fold in flour and egg whites (beaten stiff). Pour in shallow pan lined with wax paper. Bake in hot oven 12 to 15 minutes. When done turn cake out on towel which has been sprinkled with powdered sugar, add jelly and roll.

Mrs. Ray Johnson

LEBKUCHEN (German Christmas Cakes)

1 cup shortening
2 cups sugar
1 quart molasses
2 cups black coffee
2 teaspoons soda
1 ounce anise seed
½ pound citron
½ pound chopped nuts
Salt
Flour to make a stiff dough

Cream shortening and sugar. Sift soda and salt with some of the flour. Alternate liquids and flour till thoroughly mixed. Add citron and nuts while dough is soft. When dough is stiff, cool in refrigerator. Roll out a little at a time on a floured board. Cut out with oblong-shaped cutter. Bake in moderate oven till brown. When cool spread with frosting made of confectioner's sugar and ¼ cup milk. This makes a large recipe, but cookies will keep a long time.

Mrs. G. W. Hayward

ORANGE CUP CAKES

1½ cups sifted flour
2 teaspoons baking powder
¼ cup butter or substitute
¾ cup sugar
1 teaspoon grated orange rind
¼ teaspoon salt
1 egg
¼ cup evaporated milk
¼ cup orange juice

Sift flour, measure, add baking powder and salt, sift together. Cream butter with orange rind, add sugar slowly and cream until light and fluffy. Add egg and beat thoroughly. Add flour mixture alternately with combined milk and orange juice. Begin and end with flour. Stir after each addition until smooth. Drop into greased muffin pans, ⅔ full. Bake in oven 375° F. about 20 minutes. Remove from pans, cool, then frost. Makes 18 cakes.

ORANGE BUTTER FROSTING:

2 tablespoons butter, softened
1 tablespoon evaporated milk
2 tablespoons orange juice
½ teaspoon orange rind, grated
2 cups confectioner's sugar, sifted

Cream the butter. Combine milk, orange juice and rind, then add alternately with the sugar to the softened butter. Beat until smooth and ready to spread over cakes. To make handles for cakes, use long gum-drop sticks. Insert small piece of toothpick in each end, and push into cakes.

Mrs. Effie Willemin

MY BEST GINGERBREAD

½ cup sugar
½ cup butter and lard, mixed
1 egg
1 cup molasses
2½ cups sifted flour
1½ teaspoons soda
1 teaspoon cinnamon
1 teaspoon ginger
½ teaspoon cloves
½ teaspoon salt
1 cup hot water

Cream shortening and sugar. Add beaten egg, molasses, then dry ingredients which have been sifted together. Add hot water last and beat until smooth. (The batter is soft but makes a fine cake.) Bake in a moderate oven 35 minutes. Serve with whipped or plain cream.

Mrs. Lloyd Mishler

50th

Golden thoughts come stealing
Down memory's lane today
As on this fiftieth milestone
You linger on your way.
And as a curtain lifted,
The past is brought to view,—
The happy days and hours
Which long ago you knew.
The dear forgotten faces
Again you seem to see;
Old songs, old friends, old places
Pass by in memory.
Life's sun will soon be setting,—
The thought brings naught of pain,
For in yon Land of Gladness
There waits eternal gain.
Dear ones await up yonder
Whom you have missed so long,
And oft you long to mingle
With that triumphant throng.
But deeper far the yearning
To see His kindly face,
Who through the years has loved you,
And saved you by His grace.

Avis B. Christiansen

S. D. Gordon in his Quiet Talks on Home Ideals says, "A father and mother living together with their children, tender in their love, pure in their lives, strong in their convictions, simple and orderly in their habits, do infinitely more than presidents and governors, legislators and clergymen can do in making a strong nation."

RAISIN COOKIES

1 cup shortening
1 ½ cups sugar
3 eggs
1 teaspoon soda
¼ teaspoon nutmeg
3 cups flour
1 cup raisins or currants
½ cup hot water
Pinch of salt

Cream the shortening and sugar. Add the beaten eggs. Sift the dry ingredients together and add alternately with the hot water. Add the raisins. Drop by spoonfuls on a greased cookie sheet.

Mrs. Henry Babcock

SUGAR COOKIES

2 cups white sugar
1 cup lard
1 cup milk
1 teaspoon vanilla
½ teaspoon nutmeg
1 teaspoon soda
1 teaspoon baking powder
2 eggs
Flour to make rolled dough

1 cup white syrup may be substituted for one cup of sugar; decrease the milk then. Cream the shortening and sugar. Add beaten eggs. Sift the dry ingredients together and add alternately with the milk. Roll out, sprinkle with sugar. Place a raisin in the center of each cookie.

Mrs. John Zoodsma

MOTHER'S MOLASSES COOKIES

1 cup medium dark molasses
1 cup brown sugar
1 cup butter
½ teaspoon ginger
2 eggs
1 teaspoon baking soda
¼ cup hot water
1 teaspoon cinnamon
½ teaspoon nutmeg
1 teaspoon baking powder
Approximately 5 cups flour

Combine molasses, brown sugar, butter and ginger. Bring to boil in saucepan. Cool. Add the eggs which have been well beaten. Dissolve the soda in the hot water and add to mixture. Sift remaining spices and the baking powder with two and one-half cups of the flour and add to the mixture. Add remaining flour (more, if necessary) until dough is stiff enough to roll. Chill thoroughly. Roll to one eighth inch thickness and cut with cookie cutter. Place on greased baking sheet and bake in a 375° F. oven for twelve minutes (approximately).

BROWNIES

1 ½ cups sugar
¼ pound butter
4 eggs (well beaten)
½ cup milk
3 squares chocolate, melted, or 6 tablespoons cocoa
1 cup chopped nuts
1 ½ cups sifted flour

Cream the butter, add the sugar. Add the eggs and beat well. Add the rest of the ingredients, then beat well. Spread thin on greased or buttered cookie pan. Bake in moderate oven (350° F.) for 15 to 20 minutes. Cut in squares while still warm.

Mrs. J. W. Tenjack

FATHER'S DAY

A wise son maketh a glad father. (Prov. 10:1)

A son honoureth his father, and a servant his master. (Mal. 1:6)

Like as a father pitieth his children, so the Lord pitieth them that fear him. (Ps. 103:13)

Have we not all one father? hath not one God created us?

(Mal. 2:10)

And ye fathers, provoke not your children to wrath; but bring them up in the nurture and admonition of the Lord. (Eph. 6:4)

Hear, ye children, the instruction of a father, and attend to know understanding. For I give you good doctrine, forsake ye not my law. (Prov. 4:1, 2)

For whom the Lord loveth he correcteth; even as a father the son in whom he delighteth. (Prov. 3:12)

Thine own friend, and thy father's friend, forsake not.

(Prov. 27:10)

My son, keep thy father's commandment, and forsake not the law of thy mother; Bind them continually upon thine heart, and tie them about thy neck. When thou goest, it shall lead thee; when thou sleepest, it shall keep thee; and when thou awakest, it shall talk with thee. For the commandment is a lamp; and the law is light; and reproofs of instruction are the way of life

(Prov. 6:20-23)

❦

A FATHER'S PRAYER

Dear God, my little boy of three
Has said his nightly prayer to Thee;
Before his eyes were closed in sleep,
He asked that Thou his soul would keep.
And I, still kneeling at his bed,
My hand upon his tousled head,
Do ask, with deep humility,
That Thou, dear Lord, remember me.
Make me, kind Lord, a worthy Dad,
That I may lead this little lad
In pathways ever fair and bright,
That I may keep his steps aright.
O God, his trust must never be
Destroyed or even marred by me.
So, for the simple things he prayed
With childish voice so unafraid,
I, trembling, ask the same from Thee.
Dear Lord, kind Lord, remember me.

Exchange

83

SUGAR DROP COOKIES

1 cup shortening
1 ½ cups sugar
2 eggs
2 tablespoons milk
4 cups sifted flour
1 ½ teaspoons soda
1 ½ teaspoons cream of tartar
Pinch of salt
1 cup raisins, nuts or dates

Prepare the dough. Form in round ball, press with a glass dipped in sugar. Colored sugar may be used for variety. Bake in an oven 350°-375° F.

Mrs. Roma Leipold

OH-SO-GOOD GINGER DROP COOKIES

1 cup sorghum
1 cup sugar
1 cup lard or drippings
1 cup hot water
1 egg
1 tablespoon soda
1 teaspoon cinnamon
1 teaspoon ginger
Flour to make soft dough

Mix in the order given. Sift dry ingredients together, adding the soda and spices to a small amount of flour at first and then using as much flour as needed to make a batter that will drop from a spoon. This is a very easy cookie to make; even the children like to make them. There is no creaming or rolling.

Mrs. Wm. H. Losey

DROP COOKIES

2 cups brown sugar
1 cup shortening
2 eggs
½ teaspoon salt
½ teaspoon nutmeg
1 cup sour cream
4 ½ cups flour
1 teaspoon soda
4 teaspoons baking powder
1 cup raisins
1 cup nuts

Cream the sugar and the shortening. Add the beaten eggs. Sift the dry ingredients together, and add with the sour cream. Add the raisins and nuts. Drop by spoonfuls onto a greased cookie sheet.

Mrs. T. G. Lindsay

APPLESAUCE DROP COOKIES

½ cup shortening
1 cup sugar
1 egg
1 ¼ cups applesauce
1 cup raisins
½ cup chopped nuts
2 ½ cups flour
1 teaspoon soda
1 teaspoon cinnamon
¼ teaspoon cloves
1 teaspoon salt

Sift flour, measure and sift again with the soda, cinnamon, cloves and salt. Cream the shortening and gradually add the sugar. Beat until creamy, then add the egg and mix thoroughly. Add the sifted dry ingredients to the shortening mixture alternately with the applesauce. Add the raisins and nuts. Drop from a teaspoon onto a lightly greased cookie sheet. Bake in a hot oven (400° F.) for about 15 minutes, or until nicely browned.

"JAN HAGEL" (Imported Dutch Cookies)

½ pound butter
1 cup sugar
1 egg yolk
½ teaspoon cinnamon
2 cups flour
Egg white

Mix the dough. Spread beaten white of egg on top with crushed nuts. Bake in 375° F. oven 15 to 20 minutes. Grease cookie pan very lightly with butter only.

Mrs. G. C. Hughes

MY BEQUEST

To you, O son of mine, I cannot give
    A vast estate of wide and fertile lands;
But I can keep for you, the whilst I live,
    Unstained hands.

I have no blazoned scutcheon that insures
    Your path to eminence and worldly fame;
Longer than empty heraldry endures
    A blameless name.

I have no treasure chest of gold refined,
    No hoarded wealth of clinking, glittering pelf;
I give to you my hand, and heart, and mind—
    All of myself.

I can exert no mighty influence
    To make a place for you in men's affairs;
But lift to God in secret audience
    Unceasing prayers.

I cannot, though I would, be always near
    To guard your steps with the parental rod;
I trust your soul to Him who holds you dear,
    Your father's God.

Merrill C. Tenney
The Sunday School Times

❦

FRIENDLY CHAT

If you are my friend, you cannot be indifferent to my faults of character, any more than you can be indifferent to my sickness or suffering. But, if you wish to help me cure these faults, let them alone! Make much of my good qualities, if you can find any: And especially bless me with the encouraging sight of a better man than myself, and cheer me with a high example. I know that there are times when a sharp or gentle rebuke is in order, and that "faithful are the wounds of a friend." But the wiser doctors have lost faith in bloodletting; and they know that clumsy surgery kills more than it cures.

Charles G. Ames

PEANUT BUTTER COOKIES

1 cup brown sugar
1 cup white sugar
1 cup butter
1 cup peanut butter
1 teaspoon vanilla
2 eggs beaten
3 cups flour
2 teaspoons baking soda

Shape into balls the size of a walnut, and pat out with a fork. Bake in a moderate oven 12 to 15 minutes.

Mrs. Norman Karsten

COOKIES

½ cup butter
1 cup honey
1 egg
2 cups flour
½ teaspoon salt
½ teaspoon soda
¼ cup sour milk
¾ cup pecans
¾ cup raisins
¾ cup cherries
¾ cup dates

Cream butter and honey. Add egg, well beaten. Add sour milk alternately with sifted dry ingredients to which nut meats and fruits have been added. Drop on greased sheet and bake in a moderate oven (350° F.) until browned. I use chocolate morsels instead of fruit, and like them better. The fruit makes a nice Christmas cookie.

Mrs. A. Carlson

FRUIT BARS

1 cup shortening
1 cup brown sugar
1 cup flour
1 teaspoon soda, in the flour
2½ cups quick rolled oats
½ teaspoon salt
FILLING:
1 pound dates, or raisins
1 cup water (less water if raisins are used)
½ cup sugar

Use ⅔ of the dough in bottom of cookie sheet. Pat down. Spread the filling, which has been cooked until tender, over it. Pat the rest of the dough over the top. Bake in a slow oven about one hour, or until light brown. When cool, cut in bars. These stay moist and would be fine to send to those sailor or soldier boys.

Mrs. Lyle E. Harrison

CHOCOLATE DROP COOKIES

½ cup sugar
½ cup honey
½ cup shortening
2 eggs
½ cup sour milk
2 cups flour
1 teaspoon soda
1 teaspoon baking powder
½ teaspoon salt
2 squares chocolate, melted
1 teaspoon vanilla
¾ cup raisins
½ cup chopped nuts

Cream the shortening, add sugar and honey. Blend well together. Add unbeaten eggs, one at a time, beating well after each addition. Add melted chocolate and vanilla. Mix flour, soda, baking powder and salt, and add alternately with the sour milk. Lastly, add the raisins and chopped nuts. Drop onto buttered baking sheets and bake in a moderate oven from 12 to 15 minutes.

Mrs. Leonard Otto

WHEN A FATHER PRAYS

Build me a son, O Lord, who will be strong enough to know when he is weak, and brave enough to face himself when he is afraid; one who will be proud and unbending in honest defeat, and humble and gentle in victory.

Build me a son whose wishbone will not be where his backbone should be; a son who will know Thee—and to know himself is the foundation stone of knowledge.

Lead him, I pray, not in the path of ease and comfort, but under the stress and spur of difficulties and challenge. Here let him learn to stand up in the storm; here let him learn compassion for those who fail.

Build me a son whose heart will be clear, whose goal will be high; a son who will master himself before he seeks to master other men; one who will learn to laugh, yet never forget how to weep; one who will reach into the future, yet never forget the past.

And after all these are his, add, I pray, enough of a sense of humor, so that he may always be serious, yet never take himself too seriously. Give him humility, so that he may always remember the simplicity of true greatness, the open mind of true wisdom, the meekness of true strength.

Then, I, his father, will dare to whisper, "I have not lived in vain."

NOT BY BREAD ALONE

Our prayers were fervent,
For we craved
To know if he were really saved—
Our soldier boy, there on the brink
Of death. We dared not speak or think,
But called upon Christ's blessed name
Until at last the answer came—
"I'm writing that you, too, may share
The joy I've had in answered prayer."
That day we had no need of bread
For on God's wonders we had fed.

Mrs. E. W. Bliss
Moody Monthly

MOLASSES SPICE CRISPS

2 ½ cups sifted flour
2 teaspoons soda
2 teaspoons cloves
2 teaspoons ginger
2 teaspoons cinnamon
¾ cup shortening
1 cup sugar
1 egg (unbeaten)
4 tablespoons molasses
Sugar

Sift flour once, measure, add soda and spices. Sift 3 times. Cream shortening; add sugar, egg. Beat. Add molasses. Then add flour gradually. Chill. Roll in small balls. Dip in sugar. Place on ungreased baking sheet. Bake 15-20 minutes in a 350° F. oven. Very good.

Miss Effie Bouwman

MOLASSES OATMEAL COOKIES

½ cup sugar
½ cup molasses
¾ cup shortening, melted and cooled
¼ cup milk
2 eggs
2 cups sifted flour
1 teaspoon salt
½ teaspoon soda
1 teaspoon cloves
1 teaspoon cinnamon
2 cups quick oatmeal
1 cup seedless raisins

Mix the first five ingredients in the order given. Add sifted dry ingredients, oatmeal and raisins. Mix well. Drop by teaspoon on greased cookie sheet, 1 inch apart. Bake in moderate oven (375° F.) 8 to 10 minutes.

Mrs. Seymour C. Clarke

SWEDISH PEPPARKAKOR

½ pound butter
1 ½ cups sugar
1 beaten egg
2 tablespoons dark syrup
3 ¾ cups flour
2 teaspoons soda
1 teaspoon cinnamon
1 teaspoon cloves
1 teaspoon ginger
1 teaspoon cardamon

Cream the butter and sugar. Add the beaten egg and the syrup. Sift the flour with the other dry ingredients, add to the first mixture, and mix well. Let the dough stand in the icebox over night. Roll very thin in the morning, cut out in various shapes, and bake for 10-15 minutes at 375° F. I usually take a small amount at a time from the icebox and roll out all of it before baking. More spices may be added if desired. Makes over 100 thin cookies.

Mrs. Herman G. Nelson

COCOANUT COOKIES

½ cup butter
½ cup light brown sugar
1 cup bread flour
2 eggs, beaten
1 cup light brown sugar
1 cup pecan nut meats, cut fine
1 teaspoon vanilla
1 ½ cups dry cocoanut
¼ teaspoon salt
3 tablespoons flour

Cream the butter, add the sugar and blend thoroughly. Add flour. Mix and spread in 8x10-inch baking pan. Bake in 375° F. oven for 10 minutes. Beat eggs lightly and to them add all remaining ingredients. Mix thoroughly. Then pour this mixture over mixture which has been baked. Replace in oven and bake 20 minutes longer. When cooled slightly, cut in small squares for serving.

Mrs. Louise Hill

SUSAN GOES TO SCHOOL

She's gone to school, my Susan,
　So tiny, just turned six,
And, oh, the house is empty,
　The clock, how loud it ticks!
No laughter in the garden,
　No swinging on the gate,
Just quietness and order
　And a fire upon the grate.

She's gone to school, my Susan,
　In brand new pinafore,
To learn the art of letters,
　And dip in ancient lore;
She's eager for the future,
　And sturdy for her size;
But, oh, the heart is weary
　Before the head is wise!

She's gone to school, my Susan,
　So sweet and unafraid,
Her toes in shiny slippers,
　Her brown hair in a braid;
And here where she's been happy
　A little prayer I pray:
"God bless the host of Susans
　Agone to school today."

　　　　　　Vivian Yeiser Laramore

❧

Some people are making such thorough preparation for rainy
days that they aren't enjoying today's sunshine.

　　　　　　The Baptist Evangel

❧

That I Thy will may do
　Show me the way;
For this my strength renew
　From day to day;
This is my earnest plea,
Thine wholly, Lord, to be,
　And Thee obey.

DESSERTS

LEMON BISQUE

1 package lemon gelatine
1¼ cups boiling water
Juice and rind of 1 lemon
½ cup sugar, or ⅓ cup white corn syrup
1 large can evaporated milk
Any kind of fruit, and nuts, if desired
2½ cups rolled vanilla wafers

Dissolve gelatine in boiling water and add lemon juice, rind, and sugar (or corn syrup). Let mixture harden, then beat. To this add beaten condensed milk, nuts and fruit. If the can of milk is kept cold it will beat more readily. On the bottom of an oblong cake tin sprinkle ½ of the rolled wafers, pour in the above mixture and on top of that sprinkle the remainder of the wafer crumbs. Let stand in refrigerator over night. To serve, cut in squares.

PINEAPPLE MOUNDS

½ pound marshmallows (cut in pieces)
½ cup grated pineapple
½ pint cream
½ cup nuts
¾ cup graham cracker crumbs

Drain the pineapple and add the marshmallows. Let stand ½ hour. Whip the cream and fold into the pineapple mixture. Let stand for ½ hour. Add the nut meats. Let the entire mixture stand another ½ hour. Drop the pineapple mixture in mounds in the cracker crumbs. Place the cracker covered mounds on wax paper and set in the ice box until ready to serve.

Mrs. H. Nauta

APPLE CRISPETT

1 quart apples
½ cup water
¾ cup white sugar
¾ cup brown sugar
1 cup flour
5 tablespoons butter

Peel and slice the apples, and pour the water over them. Mix the other ingredients as for pie crust, and pour over the apples and water. Do not stir together. Bake in a shallow pan 45 minutes. When cool, cut in squares and serve with ice cream, or whipped cream.

Mrs. D. Benton

CHERRY COBBLER

1 can sour pitted cherries
⅔ cup sugar
2 teaspoons flour
1 tablespoon water
1 cup flour
1 teaspoon baking powder
¼ teaspoon salt
1 tablespoon sugar
2 tablespoons butter
6 tablespoons milk

Mix the cherries, sugar and flour. Allow to stand five minutes. Add the water. Pour the mixture into a deep glass or china baking dish. Mix and sift the flour, baking powder, salt and sugar. Cut in the butter with a knife. Add the milk, mixing until a soft dough is formed. Shape it with the hands to fit over the cherries. Make three slits in the dough to permit the steam to escape. Place in a 350° F. oven and bake for 30 minutes. Serve in the baking dish. Plain cream or whipped cream should be served with the cobbler.

Mrs. Albert Coleman

"IF I WERE A MOTHER"

During World War II, I was on a train traveling from Chicago to an eastern city. In the dining car, the steward seated a sailor next to me and very soon we were engaged in conversation. I discovered that the young man had just finished boot training and was on his way home for a short furlough. He had gone directly from high school into the Navy, and told me enthusiastically that he was liking it.

In the course of our conversation he said, "But, you know, there are some fellows who don't like it. They hate to take orders, they hate discipline." He went on to say, "I'm awfully glad that my parents taught me to obey. I'm thankful that they disciplined me." He looked at me rather abashedly and said, "You know, I'm a preacher's kid and I used to think my parents were awful strict, but I'm glad now that they were. The boys who had the toughest time in boot training were the fellows who had not been made to obey."

I said to him, "Will you do me a favor? When you get home tell your parents what you have told me." His reply was, "Sure. That's just what I'm going to do."

I can well imagine the mother of that youngster, who must have grieved often because he seemed to resent her correction, being grateful and proud now, because her careful, painful, diligent training was standing him in good stead—was helping him face life and endure hardness. And he is not the only boy, and she not the sole mother having this kind of experience today. Not one but many boys are hating the discipline of life, and many a girl is resenting the discipline of life, because some mother did not take her stewardship of motherhood as seriously as she ought.

I'd like to say some things right from my heart to yours, based on the thought, "If I were a mother." It has been my privilege to work with many young people as a Y.W.C.A. secretary, as a school teacher in both public and private schools, in years of summer camp work, and now as superintendent of women at the Moody Bible Institute. More than once I have had to try to take the place of an absent mother. I've learned a great deal.

Permit me to offer some suggestions to you mothers. They come not as fanciful theories from my own imagination, but have rather been gathered from what these young people, especially young women, have said to me as I have gone through all kinds of experiences with them.

If I were a mother—

I'd make the job a full-time one. I'd concentrate on bringing up my family. It would be a sacrifice, but it's a God-given responsibility, and it would be mine—along with my husband and no one else. Others may contribute—individuals, the church, the school, the Sunday school, but it would be my responsibility first and foremost. Let me appeal to you, mother, to gather your children around you. Teach them the great principles of living; read the Bible and pray with them. At first you may feel awkward when you kneel with them beside the bed, but soon the awkwardness will leave, and in its place will come blessing and enrichment to your own life, and benefit to the lives of your children.

SUET PUDDING

1 egg
1 cup sugar
¼ teaspoon cloves
¼ teaspoon allspice
1 teaspoon cinnamon
1 cup suet, chopped fine
1 cup sweet milk
½ cup raisins
2 heaping teaspoons baking
  powder
¾ teaspoon vanilla
Flour
¾ teaspoon salt

Combine the ingredients, using enough flour to mix soft. Tie in a cloth and steam 1 hour. Serve warm with any preferred sauce.

Mrs. T. G. Lindsay

BREAD PUDDING

2 cups fresh bread, broken
2 eggs
2 cups milk
½ cup sugar
2 teaspoons cocoa
½ teaspoon salt
1 teaspoon vanilla
2 tablespoons melted butter

Beat eggs. Add milk, sugar, salt, vanilla, butter, and cocoa. Pour over the broken bread. Stir until all is well mixed. Bake in moderate oven until very light, about ¾ of an hour.

Mrs. Fred Wassman

ENGLISH PLUM·PUDDING

1 pound chopped suet
2 pounds raisins
1 pound currants
1 pound mixed peel
2 cups flour
2 cups crumbs
1 teaspoon mixed spices
8 eggs
2 cups brown sugar

Mix the suet, the fruit and the chopped peel, dredge with some of the measured flour. Mix together the remaining flour, crumbs, spices and sugar, then add the well-beaten eggs. Stir fruit and suet into this mixture and mix *ALL* thoroughly. Put into greased molds or into pudding cloths. Drop into a kettle of boiling water and boil 5 to 7 hours, according to the size of the pudding. Serve with hard sauce.

Mrs. Effie Willemin

SOUR MILK PUDDING (French Recipe)

1 quart sour milk
3 eggs
2 tablespoons powdered sugar
1 tablespoon lemon juice
4 tablespoons granulated sugar

Heat the milk slowly until it separates, drain the whey from the curd. Add the eggs, powdered sugar, and lemon juice to the curd and beat thoroughly. Caramelize the granulated sugar (slowly heat, or melt sugar, until dark brown, then add 4 tablespoons boiling water and cook slowly until a thick syrup is formed) and pour it into a mold. A glass dish is excellent. Add the curd mixture and bake for 25 minutes.

Mrs. Effie Willemin

ICE BOX PUDDING

½ cup butter
1 cup powdered sugar
3 egg yolks
3 egg whites, beaten
½ pound vanilla wafers
½ cup chopped nut meats
1 teaspoon vanilla

Cream the butter and sugar together thoroughly. Add the egg yolks and beat vigorously. Add the vanilla. Fold in the stiffly beaten egg whites. Roll vanilla wafers. Put layer of wafers in pan and cover with filling, then a layer of remaining wafers. Sprinkle nuts on top. Let stand in refrigerator 24 hours.

Mrs. Virdie Marsh

I'd start to train my child at birth to obey. A child that is early taught to respect his parents' authority is much more likely to respond in obedience to God and to others in authority over him.

I'd study to win the confidence of my child. I would encourage, but not demand, confidences. I wouldn't pry or snoop, or be obviously curious. I would patiently wait and be ready in heart and mind to receive the intimacies when they come. I would strive to be understanding and sympathetic, intelligent and reasonable. I would repeatedly remind myself that I was young once. And I would want to remember that the world in which children today are being reared is different, worse in a thousand ways than the world which I knew as a child. Many a young person has said to me, "I wish I could talk to my mother as I have talked to you, Miss Dantuma. And I wish my mother had talked to me long ago as you have." I can hear some mother say, "But my girl won't let me talk to her." I grant you there are difficulties and barriers, but you must do your part in earning the wonderful privilege of companionship with your children. They need you as a friend and counselor.

I'd try to be a good disciplinarian. So many shrink from wanting to discipline because that word to them means only inflicting punishment for wrongdoing. Discipline includes setting a standard of living, and instructing and helping a child to live up to that standard, which to Christian mothers is God's standard—plainly revealed in His Holy Word. It is a glorious privilege, for it is a part of God's plan to mold the character of your child to conform the life that you love so profoundly, into the image of the Lord Jesus Christ. Accept the challenge of it and know the joy of reaping a good harvest in the life of that dear one.

I'd strive to live a well-disciplined life myself in the fear of the Lord. I'd endeavor to be an ideal—I'd ask God to help me to be a good example. That means for you, mother, a close walk with God, a dependence on Him, a yieldedness to His will.

One day in teaching a class of college-level students, I dwelt on the Scripture injunction that children must obey their parents. I stated that the Bible teaches that one of the sins characterizing the last days is disobedience to parents, and I deplored the fact that this was very evident today. A young man in the class arose quickly and said, "It isn't all the fault of the children; parents are to blame." Too true, too often true!

God says, "children, obey your parents in the Lord: for this is right. Honor thy father and mother; which is the first commandment with promise." But let us hasten to read on, "And, ye fathers, provoke not your children to wrath: but bring them up in the nurture and admonition of the Lord" (Eph. 6:1,2,4).

Mothers, yours is the grandest, biggest, most important job in the world. And God will supply wisdom, grace, and courage sufficient to do it acceptably and well-pleasing to Him.

Miss Angelyn Dantuma, Moody Monthly

MOCK ICE CREAM

1 package gelatine
1 cup cold water
2 tablespoons brown sugar
1 pint milk
1 tablespoon vanilla
½ pint whipping cream

Dissolve gelatine in cold water. (Place in pan of hot water to dissolve.) Add sugar, milk, vanilla and whipped cream. Place in refrigerator until congealed. Grapenuts or ground nuts may be sprinkled over top. (A favorite dessert with students of the Moody Bible Institute.)

ICE CREAM

2 eggs, beaten
1 cup milk
1 cup corn syrup
1 cup whipped cream

Add the milk to the beaten eggs, add the corn syrup and the whipped cream. Pour into a freezing tray. Freeze until the mixture is solid about one inch from the edge of the freezing tray. Remove and beat thoroughly. Return to the tray and continue freezing. This recipe makes 8 servings.

Mrs. Richard N. Johnson

PINEAPPLE SHERBET

2 cups buttermilk
1 cup crushed pineapple
Juice of ½ lemon
⅔ cups sugar
1 teaspoon vanilla
1 egg white, beaten stiff

To other well mixed ingredients fold in egg white, chill and freeze in automatic refrigerator. Stir once while freezing.

L. Bourne

"SEA FOAM" (Candy)

3 cups white sugar
¾ cup white corn syrup
¾ cup hot water
3 egg whites
Vanilla
Nuts

Cook sugar, syrup and water until it spins a thread, or until it forms a hard ball in cold water. Pour it slowly into the stiffly beaten egg whites, add the vanilla and nuts, but not too soon. Stir until it is ready to drop by teaspoonfuls on a buttered platter. Fruit coloring in small amounts may be added for variety.

Mrs. John Holland

VANILLA CARAMELS

2 cups sugar
1 can light corn syrup
¼ pound butter
1 can "Carnation" milk
1 cup nutmeats
1 teaspoon vanilla
1 pinch salt

Mix sugar, syrup, butter, and salt together in saucepan, place over heat and bring to boil. When boiling point is reached, stir until the mixture is of a clear thick consistency (about fifteen or twenty minutes—this varies with the intensity of the heat). Add milk in steady stream stirring all the while; continue to cook and stir until a sample forms the consistency you prefer in cold water. The cooking time after the milk has been added is approximately twenty to twenty-five minutes. Remove from the fire and add nutmeats and vanilla. Pour into a well-greased 11x7-inch pan and cool. Turn out on greased board and cut.

Lilla Steenson

94

THANK GOD FOR HOME

"I cannot thank Thee, God, enough
For this small plot of ground, this roof,
These lifted walls that close me in
And hold me tenderly; this proof
Of Thy kind care for my great need
Of shelter and of daily bread;
But oh, there are no written words,
There are no words that have been said
That could express my gratitude
For the companionship of Love
That shares my simple fare—dear God,
A gift I would be worthy of!
And I would thank Thee for the tasks;
A fire to tend, a loaf to bake;
A floor to sweep, a seam to sew,
A clean, white-sheeted bed to make,
A lamp to light at evening time—
I thank Thee, God, for all of these:
For home, my home—for every home—
I thank Thee, God, upon my knees."

Grace Noll Crowell
Light of the Years
Harper and Brothers

The Psalmist said: "What shall I render unto the Lord for all his benefits toward me? I will offer to Thee the sacrifice of thanksgiving." "Bless the Lord, O my soul, and forget not all his benefits; who forgiveth all thine iniquities; who healeth all Thy diseases; who redeemeth thy life from destruction; who crowneth thee with loving-kindness and tender mercies; who satisfieth thy mouth with good things; so that thy youth is renewed like the eagles" (Psa. 103:2-5). "O give thanks unto the Lord; call upon his name: make known his deeds among the people. Declare his glory among the heathen, his wonder among all people."

ICE BOX PIE CRUST

½ pound lard
Pinch of salt
½ cup boiling water
3 cups flour, sifted
½ teaspoon baking powder

Pour the water over lard. Stir until creamy. Add the flour and baking powder. Form a ball and let cool before rolling out. (Can be stored in refrigerator.)

Mrs. Harry Ohlson

ONE CRUST PIE SHELL

1 ¼ cups sifted flour
½ teaspoon salt
Pinch of baking powder
5 ½ tablespoons shortening
3 tablespoons cold water

Blend first three ingredients until they are the consistency of fine meal. Add water till it clings together. Roll out. Prick entire crust with fork before putting on the tin.

Mrs. Alvin Anderson

PECAN PIE

3 eggs, slightly beaten
1 cup Karo (blue label)
⅛ teaspoon salt
1 teaspoon vanilla
1 cup sugar
⅔ cup pecan meats

Mix all ingredients together, adding nutmeats last. Pour into pastry lined plate. Bake in a hot oven (450° F.) 10 minutes, then reduce heat to moderate (350° F.), and continue baking until a silver knife blade inserted in center of filling comes out clean.

PUMPKIN PIE

1 cup pumpkin
1 cup sugar
½ teaspoon salt
1 egg, well beaten, add
1 cup milk
½ teaspoon cinnamon
½ teaspoon ginger

Mix together ingredients, and taste for proper flavor before pouring into unbaked pie shell. Sprinkle nutmeg over top. Bake in moderate oven.

Mrs. Nicholas G. Prester

RHUBARB PIE DELUXE

2 cups cooked rhubarb
½ cup sugar
Vanilla
2 egg yolks
1 heaping tablespoon cornstarch

MERINGUE:
2 egg whites
2 tablespoons powdered sugar
Pinch of baking powder

Boil all together until thick, and pour into baked pie shell. Cover with meringue made with 2 egg whites, 2 tablespoons powdered sugar and a pinch of baking powder. Brown in oven.

Mrs. Harry Ohlson

WHAT DO RELIGIONS OFFER WOMANHOOD?

BUDDHISM looks at woman thus: "Just as when the disease called mildew falls upon the field of rice in fine condition, that field of rice does not continue long; just so under whatsoever doctrine and discipline women are allowed that religion will not last long. Bad conduct is the taint of women. Verily, the life of women is always darkness."

MOHAMMEDANISM: "Men are superior to women on account of the qualities which God hath gifted the one above the other. Ye may divorce your wives twice; and then either retain them with humanity or dismiss them with kindness. Of other women who seem good to your eyes, take two, or three, or four."

CONFUCIANISM: "The Master said, 'Of all people, girls and servants are the most difficult to behave to. If you are familiar with them, they lose their humility. If you maintain a reserve toward them, they are discontented. The woman follows and obeys the man. In her youth she follows her father and elder brother. When married, she follows her son.' "

HINDUISM: "With women there can be no lasting friendship; hearts of hyenas are the hearts to women. The husband should not eat in the presence of his wife. Such indeed is the divine ordinance. Women, the low-caste Sundre, the dog, the blow crow, are untruth. Stealing grain, base metals, or cattle, slaying women and low-caste Sundres, and atheism are all minor offenses."

But now let us see *what Christ has done* for woman. "He who made them from the beginning made them male and female, and said: For this cause a man shall leave his father and mother, and shall cleave to his wife: and the two shall become one flesh. So that they are no more two, but one flesh. What therefore God hath joined together, let no man put asunder. There is neither Jew nor Greek, there is neither bond nor free, there is neither male nor female in Christ Jesus."

Christian women, would you exchange your Christ for any other religion? Then, do you owe anything to the One who made your exalted position possible? Christian men, are you glad that your mothers and sisters are not held down in a hopeless heathen bondage? The woman in a Christian land enjoys the loftiest position of her sex.

DEEP DISH CHERRY PIE

½ pound American cheese
¼ cup shortening
2 cups flour
½ teaspoon salt
2 tablespoons cold water
4 tablespoons minute tapioca
1 cup sugar
3 tablespoons melted butter or margarine
4 cups canned pitted sour red cherries with juice

Blend the cheese (softened at room temperature) and the shortening. Work in the flour and salt. Add water to form a dough. Chill.

Combine the tapioca, sugar, melted butter or margarine, cherries and juice. Let stand for an hour, then mix well, and pour into a shallow baking dish—about 9 x 6 x 2 inches. Roll the pastry ¼-inch thick, and make several slits in it with a sharp knife, to permit steam to escape. Place the pastry over the cherry mixture, and press it well down over the edges of the baking dish, then trim as for a pie. Bake in a hot oven (450° F.) 15 minutes, then reduce the heat to a moderate oven (350° F.), and bake 25 to 30 minutes, or until the pastry is well baked and lightly browned.

BUTTERSCOTCH PIE

3 tablespoons butter
6 tablespoons flour
¾ cup brown sugar
¼ teaspoon salt
2 cups milk
2 eggs
½ teaspoon vanilla

Cream butter and flour together. Add brown sugar and salt. Pour milk on gradually, beating. Cook in double boiler 15 minutes, stirring constantly. Add egg yolks well beaten. Cool slightly. Add vanilla. Pour into baked shell. Top with meringue made with stiffly beaten egg whites and sugar. Brown in oven (325° F.) for 20 minutes.

Mrs. Oscar Green

SOURED CREAM COCOANUT PIE

3 egg yolks
½ cup sugar
¼ teaspoon salt
1 tablespoon flour
¼ teaspoon cinnamon
2 teaspoons vanilla
1 cup soured cream
1 can moist cocoanut—4 ounces

Beat egg yolks, sugar, and salt together with a rotary beater for five minutes. Combine flour and cinnamon and add to egg yolk mixture. Mix soured cream, cocoanut and vanilla together and add. Pour into an unbaked pie shell. Bake on a rack placed in the lowest groove in a 450° F. oven for 10 minutes, then reduce heat to 300° F. Raise rack to the center and continue to bake for 20 to 25 minutes or until filling shrinks a little from the crust and is puffed and lightly browned. Top with brown sugar meringue (your regular meringue recipe, but use brown sugar and rub it through a sieve).

LEMON SPONGE PIE

1 egg white
2 tablespoons flour
½ tablespoon corn starch
¼ teaspoon salt
1 cup sugar
Juice and grated rind of 1 lemon
1 cup milk
3 egg yolks
2 egg whites

Line the pie pan with pastry. Beat the white of 1 egg slightly and spread over the top of the pastry. For the filling, mix the dry ingredients. Then mix the lemon rind and juice with the milk and well-beaten egg yolks. Mix the liquid into the dry ingredients, then add stiffly beaten egg whites. Bake at 425° F. for 15 minutes, then at 325° F. for 30 minutes.

Mrs. Titus Miller

MOTHER'S MOLASSES COOKIES, See Page 82

Courtesy Bowman Dairy Co.

Courtesy Kraft Cheese Co.

DEEP DISH CHERRY PIE, See Page 98 ➡

▲ SOURED CREAM COCOANUT PIE, See Page 98

Courtesy Bowman Dairy Co.

Courtesy Bowman Dairy Co.

PUMPKIN PIE, See Page 96

EVERLASTING LOVE

Loved with everlasting love,
Led by grace that love to know;
Spirit, breathing from above,
Thou hast taught me it is so!
Oh, this full and perfect peace!
Oh, this transport all divine;
In a love which cannot cease,
I am His and He is mine.

Heaven above is softer blue,
Earth around is sweeter green!
Something lives in every hue
Christless eyes have never seen:
Birds with gladder songs o'er flow,
Flowers with deeper beauties shine,
Since I know, as now I know,
I am His, and He is mine.

Things that once were wild alarms
Cannot now disturb my rest;
Closed in everlasting arms,
Pillowed on the loving breast.
Oh, to lie forever here,
Doubt and care and self resign,
While He whispers in my ear—
I am His, and He is mine.

His forever, only His;
Who the Lord and me shall part?
Ah, with what a rest of bliss
Christ can fill the loving heart!
Heaven and earth may fade and flee,
First-born light in gloom decline;
But, while God and I shall be,
I am His and He is mine.

Rev. J. Mountain

GALINHA ITALAHARINI
Latin-American Dish meaning Chicken and Noodles

1 chicken, size depending upon
   how many are to be served
1 package noodles
1 green pepper
1 onion
1 can tomato soup
1 can mushroom soup
1 can Parmesan cheese

Have chicken cut up as for fricassee. Season to taste, brown quickly in hot fat. Let simmer in closely covered kettle to which has been added a little water. Cook until chicken is tender. Boil noodles until tender.

Sauce: Slightly brown onion and green pepper in a little chicken fat. To this add a can of tomato soup and a can of mushroom soup, add enough water to make a creamy sauce. Serve by placing a layer of noodles on a deep platter; over the noodles pour some of the gravy; sprinkle with cheese. The pieces of chicken are placed around the outside of the platter.

Mrs. Ethel Tylee

MU HSU JOU

½ pound lean pork, sliced fine
1 bunch spinach, cut in pieces
4 beaten eggs
12 mushrooms (if dry soak in hot
   water 5 minutes)

SAUCE:
3 tablespoons soy sauce
1 teaspoon corn starch
½ teaspoon salt
3 tablespoons water

Put lard in the skillet. When hot, cook pork in it for about 10 minutes. Take out pork and cook the eggs two or three minutes. Remove them. Now cook the mushrooms and spinach together for 8 to 10 minutes. Return all to the skillet and re-heat. Make the sauce, and pour over the cooked dish. Serve very hot.

Mrs. K. T. Ch'i

BHUGIA (Indian Dish)

2 cups peas
4 medium potatoes
1 large green pepper, chopped
2 tablespoons oil or melted fat
1 teaspoon salt

Boil peas and potatoes separately. When done, drain, cool potatoes so they are easily handled. Slice and saute potatoes and peas in the hot oil or fat. Season with salt, and sprinkle with chopped green pepper. Simple, but good.

Mrs. Effie Willemin

NORWEGIAN MEAT BALLS

1 pound round steak, ground
1 pound pork, ground
1 teaspoon ginger
½ teaspoon cloves
½ teaspoon cinnamon
1 large onion, minced
3 tablespoons milk
Salt and pepper

Mix ingredients well. Let stand for 2½ hours. Make into balls the size of a walnut and fry in hot lard. Cover while frying.

Mrs. Doris Landers

100

MISSIONARY PAGE

Go ye into all the world, and preach the gospel to every creature.
(Mark 16:15)

Now then we are ambassadors for Christ, as though God did beseech you by us: we pray you in Christ's stead, be ye reconciled to God. (II Corinthians 5:20)

Wherever there are lost souls, that place is a mission field. You may not be able to go to the foreign mission field to reach men and women, boys and girls for Christ, but right where you are is your mission field. What about that next door neighbor? What about the milkman? What about the grocer, the butcher? Remember that "man cannot live by bread alone"—be a missionary!

Robert E. Speer tells the story of a boy at Yale who inherited a small fortune. Not wanting to waste it he went to one of his old friends, a wise and successful man, and asked him for his advice. How should he invest his life and this money of his?

"My son," said the old man, "I will tell you what to do. Attach yourself to one of the great feeding interests. Don't manufacture things that can be dispensed with. There will come times when men will give up their luxuries, but there will never come a time when men will not have to eat. And if you want to be identified with one of the secure interests of mankind, attach yourself to one of those which feed the hunger of the world."

That is more than good business advice. It is a Christian challenge. The world is hungry. Feed it!

But there is a greater hunger than the hunger for bread. It is the hunger of the soul for Christ, the Living Bread; and two-thirds of all who die, die in that hunger—without Him. 26,000,000 a year, 3000 every hour! That is the greatest single need in the world today. Will you give your life to it—give your life to feeding the hunger of the world? Jesus said, "Feed my sheep."

The famine of the Word of God as mentioned in Amos 8:11, 12, 13, is very evident now and we who feast upon the Bible are called to allow the Holy spirit to use us as Silver Trays to present CHRIST, the Bread of Life, to millions NOW.

Samuel Hugh Moffett of Student Foreign Mission Fellowship

SWEDISH LIMPA (Bread)

2 cups water
¼ cup brown sugar
¼ cup honey
1½ teaspoons caraway seed
1 teaspoon anise seed
1 tablespoon lard
2 yeast cakes
4 cups white flour
1 teaspoon salt
2 cups rye flour

Heat together water, sugar, honey, spices and lard. Cool to lukewarm, add yeast, mix well. Add about 3 cups of the white flour, beat thoroughly, add rye flour, salt and more white flour, make a dough that can be easily handled. Turn out on floured board, and knead until satiny or elastic. Place dough in a greased bowl, grease top of dough, let rise double in size (2 to 4 hours). Knead, shape into loaves, put into greased pans; brush top with melted shortening, cover. Let rise again (1 to 2 hours). Bake 20 minutes in 400° F. oven. Reduce heat to 350° F. and bake 40 minutes longer. Excellent for mid-afternoon lunch.

Mrs. Effie L. Willemin

SCOTCH SCONES

2 cups flour
¼ teaspoon salt
1 teaspoon baking powder
¼ teaspoon baking soda
1 teaspoon sugar
1 egg
1 cup sour milk

Mix dry ingredients, sift, and combine with beaten egg and milk. Put on floured board and cut in small squares. Bake in floured pan on top of stove.

Mrs. John Fleeton

FROZEN KOLACKY (Bohemian Recipe)

½ pound butter, sweet or salted
1 small bottle sweet cream
2 teaspoons sugar
1 teaspoon nutmeg
3 eggs—omit the yolk of one egg
1 cake yeast
Flour to make a heavy dough

Mix cream and butter together. Add the other ingredients. Then crumble a cake of yeast into mixture. Add enough flour to make a heavy dough. Let stand over night in refrigerator. Roll out dough to about ½-inch thickness. Then cut with small cookie cutter. Put on dry pans and spread with chopped prunes or other fruit. Let stand until raised. Bake in a 400° F. oven.

Virginia Goldberger

DUTCH BABBELAARS (Holland Recipe)

2 pounds light brown sugar
¼ cup vinegar
½ cup water
Butter (size of walnut)

Stir enough to mix well and put on fire to cook. Watch closely so it will not burn. Test in cold water. When it reaches the hard ball stage, remove from the fire and pour in buttered pan and let cool enough so it can be handled. Pull like taffy and cut in small pieces. (This is very good and an excellent candy to pack for some soldier boy.)

Mrs. H. Nauta

A HEATHEN WOMAN'S FACE

Have you ever read the sorrow in a heathen woman's face,
  As you met her eye to eye amid a throng?
She who is by sex your sister, though of different race,
  Have you ever wondered why she has no song?
It will take no occult power to fathom all her secrets deep,
  And it needs no cruel probing just to know;
If you're filled with Christ's compassion and can weep with those
    who weep,
  All her inmost soul will then to you outflow.
If you let Christ's love flow through you with a power she can feel,
  She will follow close behind you as you go;
And if you but turn a moment, you will meet her mute appeal
  For a blessing that your shadow might bestow.
Yes, she feels *you* bear the comfort she has sought for years to find,
  In the temple, where her gods sit row on row,
And somehow your very presence breathes a balm for troubled
    mind,
  For she feels that you must understand and know.

. . . .

She's a prisoner that beats against the very bars of life,
  And she longs for death, yet dares not, must not die.
She is cursed with cruel curses should she be a sonless wife,
  And a baby daughter answer cry with cry.
She's the common drudge of yesterday and dreads the cruel mor-
    row,
  While today the weary hours drag like a chain.
And she prays to gods all deafened to her tale of sin and sorrow,
  Or if they hear, are heedless of her pain.
She's the daughter of her mother, who before her trod the road.
  She's the mother of a daughter who will know
All the depths of her own anguish, all the heavy, weary load,
  All the bitterness—a heathen woman's woe!
No, 'tis not a heathen woman—'tis a piteous captive throng,
  In the deserts, jungles, paddy fields and marts,
In the lands that know not Jesus, lands of cuelty and wrong,
  Where there is no balm for wounded, aching hearts.
Shall we let this stream flow downward in its widening, deathward
    way?
  Shall we let this flood of misery hold its throng?
We can stem the deadly current if we go and give and pray—
  They must join us in the glad redemption song!
              Mrs. W. M. Turnbull, Alliance Weekly

CHILDREN'S RECIPES

• RULES FOR LITTLE COOKS •

Read the recipe carefully.
Hands must be scrubbed clean.
Now put on your apron.
Place all utensils you will need on the kitchen work table.
Mother will show you how to light and regulate the oven.
All measurements must be accurate.
Baking dishes must be washed, dried, and put away.
Sweep kitchen and leave it in order.
Level all dry ingredients like this.

FAIRY GINGERBREAD

1 cup sugar

½ cup butter

2 eggs

1 cup milk

1 cup molasses

2½ cups flour

½ teaspoon soda

1 tablespoon ginger

Cream sugar and butter in a bowl. Beat eggs, then add milk and molasses. Sift flour, soda, and ginger into mixture and beat well. Bake in shallow greased pan in moderate oven (350° F.) for 45 minutes.

CHOO-CHOO SALAD

4 large raw carrots

1 cup raisins

1 tablespoon orange juice

Lettuce

Grind carrots and raisins through food chopper. Mix with orange juice. Serve on crisp lettuce leaf.

CHILDREN'S DAY
Home Influence

A child can read a parent's character before he knows the alphabet. Home is the station of greatest responsibility. The child is the canvas upon which the father and mother paint their own portraits. "I'll take what father takes" was a boy's unconscious testimony to the truth of this principle. Parental and family ties form one of the most potent means God uses in converting souls. Home is the nearest and most promising field of Christian service. Nowhere will consistent Christian living and godly example go so far as there. We must bear in mind that home life is the best test of Christian character. Home is the hardest place to play the hypocrite. A godly home life is one of the best proofs of a true hope in Jesus Christ.

Let the family altar be strengthened. Let our homes be like the home in Bethany, where Jesus loved to be a guest. Let kindness, gentleness, and forbearing love make home more dear and precious. Keep the atmosphere pure and sweet. Do not reserve your best looks and kindest words for strangers, but make home brighter by them. Thus "home" may be made "heaven" on earth, as God intended every home to be.

MOTHER'S INFLUENCE

I took a piece of plastic clay
And idly fashioned it one day,
And as my fingers pressed it still,
It moved and yielded at my will.
I came again when days were past,
The form I gave it still it bore,
But I could change that form no more.
I took a piece of living clay,
And gently formed it day by day,
And molded with my power and art,
A young child's soft and yielding heart,
I came again when days were gone,
It was a man I looked upon,
He still that early impress bore
And I could change it nevermore.

Author and source unknown

105

UNCOOKED FUDGE

1 egg
1 package confectioner's sugar
3 tablespoons cream
4 squares bitter chocolate
3 teaspoons butter

Beat egg. Stir 1 cup of sugar into egg. Add cream. Stir in rest of sugar. Melt chocolate and butter in top of double boiler over boiling water. Add to sugar, egg and cream. Spread in tin and cut in squares.

SPICY APPLE SAUCE

6 sour apples
2/3 cup sugar
1 cup water
8 whole cloves

Wash apples. Cut apples in quarters. Take out core carefully. Put apples, sugar, water, and cloves in saucepan. Cook slowly until apples are very soft. Mash through colander or strainer.

TAPIOCA PUDDING

2 cups milk
1 1/2 tablespoons minute tapioca
2 eggs
1/3 cup sugar
1 teaspoon vanilla

Heat milk and tapioca in double boiler. Stir often. Beat eggs, then mix eggs and sugar. Stir egg mixture into tapioca slowly. Cook and stir until thick or about 15 minutes. Let cool, then add vanilla. Serve plain or with cream.

OLD KING COLE SPINACH

2 eggs
2 cups cooked spinach

Beat eggs until foamy. Chop spinach fine, in chopping bowl. Mix spinach and eggs well. Pour into buttered baking dish. Bake in moderate oven (350° F.) for 1/2 hour.

A LOVE CAKE FOR MOTHER

Recipe

1 can of "Obedience"
Several pounds of "Affection"
1 pint of "Neatness"
Some Holiday, Birthday, and
    everyday "Surprises"
1 can of "Running Errands"
    (willing brand)
1 box of powdered "Get up
    when I should"
1 bottle of "Keep sunny all day
    long"
1 can of pure "Thoughtfulness"

Method

Mix well, bake in a hearty,
warm oven, and serve to "Mother" every day. She ought to
have it in Big Slices.

Jean Beadle
Age 14 years

THE PROMISED DOLLY

I promised a doll to my dear baby girl,
    I pictured a doll most fair,
With exquisite features, and teeth of pure pearl,
    Moving eyes! Walking limbs! And real hair!

We entered a shop and the dear little maid
    Clasped a cheap tawdry doll to her breast;
To make the exchange I was really afraid,
    Though I wanted to give her the best.

I took it away and the tears filled her eyes,
    Till I gave her the one I had planned.
Then the dear little face glowed with joyous surprise
    That a dolly existed so grand!

Oh, baby! I, too, am a child in *God's* sight;
    I choose the *first* things that I see.
I struggle to keep them! I don't know quite
    Why my Father should take them from me.

But when I look back through the wisdom of years
    When my faith is age-old and sublime,
Perhaps I shall see through a rainbow of tears
    That my *Father* planned *best all the time.*

Author and source unknown

COMBINATIONS FOR SANDWICHES:

Grated carrots and finely chopped peanuts, combined with salad dressing.
Peanut butter moistened with salad dressing and mixed with raisins, dates, or figs.
Cream cheese and chopped stuffed olives.
Tunafish mixed with parsely, lemon juice and seasoning.

Mrs. T. E. Miller

LIVER AND CELERY SANDWICH SPREAD

½ cup cooked liver, ground fine
¼ cup celery, chopped fine
1 tablespoon green pepper cut fine
1 tablespoon onion juice or chopped onion
1 tablespoon chopped parsley

Blend and moisten with cream or tomato juice. Yields 3-4 sandwiches.

CHEESE-PEANUT SANDWICH FILLING

¼ pound cream cheese
¼ cup peanuts
2 tablespoons salad dressing
Cream

Grind cheese and nuts through food chopper using coarse knife. Add salad dressing and enough cream to make right consistency for spreading.

BARBECUE (Delicious for Sandwiches)

1 pound lean boiling beef
1 pound lean pork
1 bunch celery
3 onions
1 tablespoon brown sugar
2 teaspoons chili powder
2 green peppers
1 cup tomato catsup
½ cup vinegar
Chop suey sauce

Cook the beef and pork together in onion water a long time, until tender enough to pull apart. As water evaporates during cooking, add more so that you will have 2 cups stock. Pull meat apart in shreds with two forks. While meat is cooking put the celery, peppers and onions through food chopper. Add to this the catsup, brown sugar, vinegar and chili powder, chop suey sauce, and salt and pepper to taste. Cook in meat stock until thick enough to spread. Add shredded meat. Any left over meats may be used and one does not need to adhere to exact proportions, but suit the taste.

Miss Talka H. Wubbena

What are children to us?
Psalm 127:3
Genesis 48:4
I Samuel 1:11
Genesis 30:1-3

Two Prayers by two Mothers
I Samuel 2
Luke 1:52, 53
Read Proverbs 8:14-36

What Children are by Nature
Proverbs 22:15
Ephesians 3
Psalm 51:5

What Children mean to God
Mark 9:37-41
Jeremiah 2:9
Mark 10:14
Luke 18:16
Psalm 90:16
Isaiah 54:13
Jonah 4:11
Matthew 18:10, 11

The Importance of Obedience
I Samuel 2:27, 36
I Samuel 3:4, 18
Deuteronomy 21:18
Colossians 3:20
Ephesians 6:2, 3

~~~

PRAYERS FOR CHILDREN

For all thy gifts we thank Thee, God:
For day and night and food,
For love of work, for play and friends;
For joy in all that's good.
E. McE. S.

Jesus, Friend of little children,
Be a friend to me;
Take my hand and ever keep me,
Close to Thee.

Teach me how to grow in goodness,
Daily as I grow,
Thou hast been a child, and surely
Thou dost know.
Amen.

Rev. W. J. Mathams

QUANTITY RECIPES

MACARONI AND CHEESE
(Serves 90 portions)

6 pounds elbow macaroni
3 pounds aged Wisconsin cheese, grated
1 medium onion, grated

SAUCE:
2½ cups shortening
2 cups flour
¼ cup mustard
¼ cup paprika
¼ cup salt
7½ quarts milk

Cook macaroni in boiling salted water (about 2 gallons) until done. Drain off water and cover with cold water. Drain, then mix with sauce and cheese.

Melt shortening, add flour and remaining dry ingredients, gradually add the scalded milk, and stir constantly. When smooth, and well cooked, remove from unit, add cheese, onion and cooked macaroni. Place macaroni mixture in electric roaster pre-heated to 350° F. for about 1 hour.

BAKED BEANS
(Serves 50 portions of ½ cup each)

5 pounds navy beans
2 tablespoons salt
1 medium sized onion
1 tablespoon (dry) mustard
½ cup molasses (or more, according to taste)
7 16-ounce cans tomato juice
2 pounds salt pork

Wash the beans and let soak over night. Pour off water and parboil for 8 to 10 minutes. Drain off water and put beans and seasonings in cold roaster. Turn the thermostat to 500° F. until boiling point is reached, then reduce the temperature to 300° F. and let cook for five hours. If time permits, allow the beans to slow bake at 200° F. for two or three hours additional time.

CHOP SUEY
(Serves 50 portions of ¾ cup each)

18 stalks celery
5 pounds Bermuda onions
5 pounds pork, cut for chop suey
3 pounds veal, cut for chop suey
6 cups water or meat stock
2½ cups cornstarch
¾ cup molasses
3½ cups Chinese sauce
6 No. 2 cans bean sprouts
1 pound fresh tomatoes
2 green peppers
1 4-ounce can pimientoes
6 pounds rice

Cook diced celery and sliced onions with water, or meat stock, until vegetables are soft, but not completely cooked. Brown meat in 2 tablespoons fat. While meat is browning, drain liquid from celery and onions, and mix with the Chinese sauce, molasses and cornstarch; cook on high until it boils, then add the meat, and let sauce continue to cook until starchy taste is gone, or about 30 minutes, at 350° F. Add the bean sprouts, which have been drained, celery and onions, let cook only until thoroughly heated, then add tomatoes, green peppers and pimientoes which have been cut in thin strips. Serve on boiled rice or Chinese fried noodles. *Note:* No salt is used in Chop Suey as the Chinese Sauce is quite salty.

A MOTHER'S PRAYER

I wash the dirt from little feet, and as I wash I pray,
"Lord, keep them ever pure and true to walk the narrow way."
I wash the dirt from little hands, and earnestly I ask,
"Lord, may they ever yielded be to do the humblest task."
I wash the dirt from little knees, and pray, "Lord, may they be
The place where victories are won, and orders sought from Thee."
I scrub the clothes that soil so soon, and pray, "Lord, may her dress
Throughout eternal ages be Thy robe of righteousness."

E'er many hours shall pass, I know, I'll wash these hands again;
And there'll be dirt upon her dress before the day shall end.
But as she journeys on through life and learns of want and pain,
Lord, keep her precious little heart cleansed from all sin and stain;
For soap and water cannot reach where Thou alone can'st see.
Her hands and feet, these I can wash—I trust her heart to Thee.

B. Ryberg, King's Business

❦

LIVING EPISTLES

The best way to preach the Gospel is to live it. At least it must be lived before it is preached, to be effective. Thus the Saviour lived the Sermon on the Mount for thirty years before He preached one word of it. And just before He died He set a Divine and final standard of life and godliness for all "them which should hereafter believe," a standard ever binding on all God's children. "I have given you," He said, "an example that ye should do as I have done to you." This was specially in regard to humility and forebearance to fellow-believers. Peter, writing later, enlarges this "example" which He left, in regard to suffering. And God would never have us content with a lower standard.

Dr. Northcote Deck
Used by permission from
The Evangelical Christian

111

SCALLOPED POTATOES
(Serves 50 portions of ½ cup each)

1 peck potatoes
1 cup flour
4 tablespoons salt
½ teaspoon pepper
2 cups butter
13 cups hot milk

Peel potatoes and slice. Put into shallow baking pan a layer of potatoes then a slight dredging of flour and repeat until potatoes are used. Dissolve salt, pepper and butter in hot milk. Pour over potatoes. Bake in oven pre-heated to 400° F. for about 1 hour.

CHICKEN A LA KING (Serves 20)

1 chicken cut fine
1 can mushrooms
¼ pound butter
¾ cup flour
1 quart milk
2 slices of pimiento
½ green pepper
1 small bunch celery
Salt
Pepper
1 teaspoon paprika

Make cream sauce, add seasonings, pimiento, green pepper. To this mixture add chicken and mushrooms.

Mrs. Cleda Smith

BOILED RICE
(Serves 50 portions of ½ cup each)

5 pounds rice
6 quarts or 24 cups water
3 tablespoons salt
¼ pound butter

Heat water, salt and butter to boiling point, add the rice which has been washed. When rice reaches the boiling point, reduce the temperature to 350° F. and continue to cook for 45 minutes or until rice is tender.

SCALLOPED TUNA FISH WITH POTATOES
(Serves 50 portions)

15 pounds potatoes
1 Bermuda onion, diced
4 12-ounce tins Tuna
1 40-ounce package frozen peas
1 small can pimientoes, diced

SAUCE:

1½ cups shortening
1½ cups flour
3½ quarts milk
1 teaspoon thyme

Wash, cook and drain potatoes, with jackets on. Peel, dice and combine with cream sauce. Cook peas and onions in ½-pound butter with ½ cup water; when tender, add to creamed potatoes. Scald Tuna and break into small pieces, stir in the potato mixture. Season with salt and pepper.

FRUIT PUNCH

2 pineapples
8 cups sugar
6 cups boiling water
2 cups tea, freshly made
10 lemons
1 dozen oranges
1 quart strawberry juice
2 cups maraschino cherries
1 bottle gingerale
6 quarts water

Grate pineapple, add the boiling water and sugar and boil 15 minutes. Add the tea and strain into punch bowl. When cold add the fruit juice, the cherries and the cold water. A short time before serving add a piece of ice and on serving add the gingerale. Strawberries, mint leaves or slices of banana may be used in the place of cherries. Makes 2½ gallons of punch.

ARE ALL THE CHILDREN IN?

I think ofttimes as the night draws nigh
   Of an old house on the hill,
Of a yard all wide and blossom-starred
   Where the children played at will.
And when the night at last came down
   Hushing the merry din,
Mother would look around and ask,
   "Are all the children in?"

'Tis many and many a year since then,
   And the old house on the hill
No longer echoes to childish feet
   And the yard is still, so still.
But I see it all, as the shadows creep
   And though many the years have been
Since then, I can hear mother ask,
   "Are all the children in?"

I wonder if when the shadows fall
   On our last short, earthly day,
When we say good-bye to the world outside,
   All tired with our childish play,
When we step out into that Other Land
   Where mother so long has been,
Will we hear her ask, just as of old,
   "Are all the children in?"

Florence Jones Hadley
The Pathfinder

JAMS and JELLIES

MARMALADE AND CONSERVE TABLE

Conserve or Marmalade	Fruit	Sugar	Preparation
CARROT MARMALADE	6 lbs.	8 lbs.	Scrape carrots and grate with coarse grater. Grate lemon rinds and squeeze juice.
GRAPEFRUIT MARMALADE	4 grapefruit 4 oranges 4 lemons	6 lbs.	Slice fruit very thin, add 2 quarts water. Let stand over night.
ORANGE MARMALADE	8 oranges (medium size) 3 lemons	5 lbs.	Slice oranges and lemon very thin using skin of 5 oranges only. Add 2 quarts water. Let stand overnight.
PINECOT MARMALADE	5½ lbs. cooked apricots (dried) 5½ lbs. cooked crushed pineapple 2 lemons	5 lbs.	Mix cooked apricots and pineapple. Add juice of lemons.
TOMATO (RED OR YELLOW) MARMALADE	7 lbs. tomatoes 2 lemons 1 ounce ginger root	6 lbs.	Peel tomatoes. Place ginger root in cheese cloth bag; mash. Slice lemon thin.
CHERRY & RAISIN CONSERVE	3 lbs. cherries 4 lbs. raisins	5 lbs.	Pit cherries and wash. Cut raisins in pieces. Add 6 cups water.
GOOSEBERRY CONSERVE	5 lbs. gooseberries 4 oranges 1½ lbs. raisins	4 lbs.	Pick and wash gooseberries, removing stems and tails. Slice oranges and chop skins.
PEACH AND PINEAPPLE CONSERVE	4 lbs. peaches chopped 2 lbs. crushed pineapple 1 orange, 1 lemon	3 lbs.	Peel and chop peaches. Squeeze lemon and orange, and grate peels.
PEACH CONSERVE	4 lbs. peaches 1 lemon	3 lbs.	Mash peeled peaches. Grate lemon rind and squeeze juice. Raisins or nuts may be added.
RHUBARB CONSERVE	3 lbs. rhubarb 2 oranges ¾ lb. raisins 1 tsp. cinnamon 1 tsp. nutmeg		Cut rhubarb in small pieces. Grate orange and squeeze juice.

ORANGE-PEACH MARMALADE

12 medium cling peaches
3 medium oranges
Rind of 1½ oranges
Sugar

Wash and peel peaches, wash oranges, remove peel from 1½ of the oranges, grind fruit, combine and measure into large preserving kettle; add equal amount of sugar. Bring to boil. Boil rapidly 25 to 30 minutes, stirring occasionally to prevent burning. Pour into sterilized jars and seal.

TEN REASONS FOR A FAMILY ALTAR

It will sweeten home life and enrich home relationship as nothing else can do.

It will dissolve all misunderstanding and relieve all friction that may enter the home.

It will hold our boys and girls to the Christian ideal and determine their lasting welfare.

It will send us forth to our work for the day, in school, home, office, store and factory, true to do our best and determined in what we do to glorify God.

It will give strength to meet bravely any disappointments and adversities as they come.

It will make us conscious through the day of the attending presence of a divine Friend and Helper.

It will hallow our friendship with our guests in the home.

It will reinforce the influence and work of the church, the church school, and agencies helping to establish the Christian ideal throughout the world.

It will encourage other homes to make a place for Christ and the church.

It will honor our Father above and express our gratitude for His mercy and blessing.

Christian Digest

❧

At the same time came the disciples unto Jesus, saying, Who is the greatest in the kingdom of heaven? And Jesus called a little child unto him, and set him in the midst of them. And said, Verily I say unto you, Except ye be converted, and become as little children, ye shall not enter into the kingdom of heaven. Whosoever therefore shall humble himself as this little child, the same is greatest in the kingdom of heaven. And whoso shall receive one such little child in my name receiveth me. But whoso shall offend one of these little ones which believe in me, it were better for him that a millstone were hanged about his neck, and that he were drowned in the depth of the sea. Woe unto the world because of offences! for it must needs be that offences come; but woe to that man by whom the offence cometh! (Matthew 18:1-7)

NEW ENGLAND APPLE MARMALADE

3 cups sugar
2½ cups water
2 oranges
5 pounds tart apples
2 lemons

Heat sugar and water together until sugar is dissolved. Slice oranges and apples very thin and add lemon juice. Add to syrup and boil very slowly until thick—about 1¼ hours to 2 hours. Turn into sterilized glasses or jars and when cool seal with paraffin.

Miss Talka H. Wubbena

GRAPE MARMALADE

Remove grapes from stems and wash. Separate skins from pulp. Cook pulp until tender. Remove seeds by pressing through sieve. Mix skins and pulp and add ¾ cup of sugar to each cupful of mixture.

Cook until skins are tender, or about 5 minutes. Test to see if it sets.

The fruit is better if not too ripe as it has more pectin and jells more quickly.

Put in sterile jars and seal while hot. It most always keeps the ripe grape color.

Miss Minnie Richards

CURRANT JELLY (SPICED)

5 pounds currants
1 ounce stick cinnamon
1 tablespoon whole cloves
Sugar

Wash currants but do not remove stems; mash slightly to start juice; cook slowly until currants look white. Drain in jelly bag. Tie spices in cheesecloth and boil in extracted juice 10 minutes. Remove spices, measure juice, and for each cup juice add ¾ cup sugar. Boil rapidly to jelly stage. Pour into sterilized jelly glasses.

TUTTI FRUIT JELLY

4 quarts red currants
4 pints red raspberries
6 oranges
1 pound seeded raisins

Pick over, wash, and cover berries with water. Cook until soft and strain through jelly bag. Add to this juice, oranges diced, skin and pulp. Add the raisins, which have been cut fine. Then measure 1 cup juice, raisin and orange mixture, and 1 cup sugar, using only three cups to a pan, and cook as you would any other jelly until it jells. This makes 24 glasses. And it is just delicious. The fruit comes to the top of the glass to make a conserve while the rest is jelly.

Lillian Wise

STRAWBERRY JAM

2 cups crushed berries
3 cups sugar

Wash and drain berries; crush and cook without water. Heat slowly and when bubbling all over add the sugar. Let boil 10 minutes and seal in jars.

Mrs. T. E. Miller

CRANBERRY JAM

4 cups fresh cranberries
1 cup water
1¼ cups sugar
1¼ cups corn syrup
1 cup ground seeded raisins
¼ cup orange juice
grated rind of 1 orange

Cook the cranberries in the water until all the skins pop open. Then put through sieve and add the sugar, syrup, raisins, and orange. Cook together for 15 minutes. Remove from heat and pack in sterilized jars or glasses and seal with paraffin immediately.

Mrs. H. C. Selstad

THERE'S A SONG IN THE AIR

There's a song in the air! There's a star in the sky!

    There's a mother's deep prayer and a baby's low cry!

And the star rains its fire while the beautiful sing,

    For the manger of Bethlehem cradles a King.

In the light of that star lie the ages impearled;

    And that song from afar has swept over the world.

Many hearths are aflame, and the beautiful sing,

    In the homes of the nations that Jesus is King.

We rejoice in the light, and we echo the song

    That comes down through the night from the heavenly throng.

Ay! we shout to the lovely evangel they bring,

    And we greet in His cradle our Saviour and King.

Dr. J. G. Holland

RHUBARB AND PINEAPPLE JAM

7 pounds rhubarb
2 medium-sized pineapples
5 pounds sugar

Chop rhubarb and pineapples into small pieces. Add half the sugar and cook 15 minutes. Then add remaining sugar and simmer, stirring often, until rich and thick. Pour into sterilized jars and seal.

CURRANT BUTTER

7 pounds currants
3 pounds sugar
1 teaspoon cinnamon (large)
½ cup sweet cider, or vinegar

Put enough water on currants as you would for jelly. Boil until currants are tender. Cool. When still warm press through sieve. Then add ingredients and boil as any other butter or jam. When ready for spread pour in sterile jars and cover with melted paraffin.

Miss Minnie Richards

HOW TO MAKE SYRUP

No. 1 THIN SYRUP

Use three parts of water or fruit juice to one part of sugar and bring to a boil. The THIN syrups are used for small, soft fruits, as sweet cherries, berries, etc.

No. 2 MEDIUM SYRUP

Use two parts water or fruit juice to one part of sugar and bring to a boil.
MEDIUM syrups are used on peaches, sour berries, acid fruits, as rhubarb, cherries, gooseberries, etc.

No. 3 HEAVY SYRUP

Use one part of water or fruit juice to one part of sugar and bring to a boil.
HEAVY syrups are used on larger sour fruits that are to be extra sweet.
White corn syrup may be used in the proportion of 1½ cups of corn syrup substituted for each cup of sugar. Honey may also be used in place of sugar. Ordinarily 1 cup honey equals 1 cup sugar.

JELLY

No. 1

Put one quart of whole berries in pan with no sugar or water—cook until done Take off stove and strain and measure, then put juice back on stove and bring to a boil. Add 1½ cups of sugar to each cup of juice. Take off fire immediately and stir until sugar is dissolved. Seal in sterilized jars.

No. 2

Same as grape jelly, except use ⅔ to ¾ as much sugar by measure as juice.

THE STAR IN GOD'S WINDOW

Sir Harry Lauder tells the following story:

One night, a man and his small son were walking slowly down the streets of a large American city. The child was delighted to see the many service stars hanging in the windows of homes—each star proudly proclaiming the fact that a son was in the service of his country. He clapped his hands excitedly as he approached each new star, and was duly impressed by those homes with more than one star in the window.

Finally they came to a wide gap between houses, through which the black velvet of the sky was clearly discernible, with the evening star shining brightly. "Oh look, Daddy," cried the little boy, "God must have given His Son, for He has a star in His window!"

For God so loved the world, that he gave his only begotten Son, that whosoever believeth in him should not perish, but have everlasting life. For God sent not his Son into the world to condemn the world; but that the world through him might be saved. (John 3:16,17)

God gave His Son that we might know
His Father heart had loved us so;
And from the heavenly home on high
Our blessed Lord came forth to die.

God gave His Son—O, holy thought
That He our foolish love had sought;
Dear Father, take this heart of mine,
And make it wholly, deeply Thine.

119

PICKLES, RELISH

CELERY PICKLES

1 bunch celery
6 or 7 green tomatoes
25 cucumbers
5 small onions
SYRUP:
4 cups vinegar
4 cups sugar
1 teaspoon mustard seed
1 teaspoon cloves
Few sticks cinnamon

Slice the vegetables and salt over night. Drain. Pour boiling water over them and let stand until yellow. Drain. Cook the syrup, add the vegetables. Let them come to a boil, seal while hot.

Mrs. C. J. Christopher

FRENCH PICKLES

1 peck green tomatoes
3 green peppers
1 large onion
2 quarts vinegar
2 quarts water
1 tablespoon cinnamon
1 tablespoon cloves
1 tablespoon black pepper
1 tablespoon white mustard seed
4 pounds sugar

Chop fine the tomatoes, peppers, and onion, or put them through a meat grinder. Add the water and 1 quart vinegar. Boil 15 minutes. Drain. Add the remaining vinegar and spices and sugar. Boil until it thickens, stirring often.

Mrs. S. J. Ekema

TURMERIC PICKLES

24 onions (size of walnut)
48 large pickles
6 cups sugar
3 teaspoons ground mustard
2 teaspoons turmeric powder
3 teaspoons celery seed
1 quart vinegar
Salt to taste

Sprinkle pickles and onions with salt and let stand one hour or more. Bring vinegar and spices to a boil. Add pickles and onions and heat to boiling point. Then put into sterilized jars to seal.

Mrs. Titus Miller

PICCALILLI

½ peck green tomatoes
6 medium onions
1 small head cabbage
2 red peppers
1 package 5c mixed spices, in a cloth bag
Vinegar

Chop all together, salt overnight, then drain and boil lightly in a half gallon vinegar. Let it remain in vinegar until the next day, drain, then boil in fresh vinegar with sugar to taste.

Mrs. C. J. Christopher

120

HUMILITY

"Humility is perfect quietness of heart. It is for me to have no trouble: never to be fretted or vexed or irritated or sore or disappointed. It is to expect nothing, to wonder at nothing that is done to me, to feel nothing done against me. It is to be at rest when nobody praises me, and when I am blamed or despised. It is to have a blessed home in the Lord, where I can go in and shut the door, and kneel to my Father in secret, and am at peace as in a deep sea of calmness when all around and above is trouble. It is the fruit of the Lord Jesus Christ's redemptive work on Calvary's Cross, manifest in those of His own who are definitely subjected to the Holy Spirit."

Andrew Murray

CHILI SAUCE

18 red tomatoes
12 apples
10 small onions
3 red sweet peppers
3 green sweet peppers
3 cups sugar
3 cups vinegar
3 tablespoons ground allspice in cloth bag
1 tablespoon salt

Grind all, add the sugar, vinegar, spice, and salt. Boil one hour or more. Can.

Mrs. Ray Johnson

PEPPER RELISH

12 red peppers
12 green peppers
2 tablespoons celery seed
2 tablespoons mustard seed
1 teaspoon salt
1 cup sugar
Vinegar

Cover with mild vinegar. Boil ¾ hour. Seal while hot in pint jars.

Mrs. S. J. Ekema

CORN RELISH

2 dozen ears of corn, cooked and cut off cob
10 medium size onions
4 green peppers (sweet)
4 red peppers (sweet)
1 tablespoon mustard seed
1 tablespoon celery seed
½ cup salt
½ cup sugar
1 ½ quarts vinegar, and a little water

Grind onions, peppers, add all ingredients and cook ½ hour. Seal hot. Makes 6 pints.

Lillian Wise

HOUSEHOLD HINTS

Spread oleomargarine on salted crackers and slightly brown in oven for a few minutes. Very good—tastes like *buttered* crackers.

For added nutrition add one or two well beaten eggs to cream soups just before taking from fire.

Add ½ cup All-Bran to your coffee cake batter for a nice variation; also to any kind of nut cake.

L. Bourne

A few drops or teaspoon of peanut butter placed in the bottom of each muffin pan before batter is added gives muffins a fine nutty flavor.

Orange or lemon juice does not produce a distinct flavor in baked goods—but grated rind of either does.

Any cleaning fluid will remove marks left on skin by adhesive tape.

To make pure celery salt put the leaves from celery into a pie plate and place in warming oven to dry. When dry, roll on a piece of paper until very fine. Put into a salt shaker and use instead of celery salt. It is fine served in soups.

To give baked apple a delightful flavor and to color and sweeten, add a few cinnamon drop candies. Remove core from bud end but do not cut clear through; this keeps the candies in the apple.

To one pound of butter, gradually cream in one tall can of evaporated milk and a little salt. Chill and you have two pounds of delicious spread.

Mrs. J. H. Seyller

VICTORY GARDENS

Gardens figure prominently in the Scripture. "The Lord God planted a garden eastward in Eden; and there He put the man whom He had formed" (Gen. 2:8). Thus man's first home was in a place of beauty and usefulness, for he was put "into the garden of Eden to dress it and to keep it" (Gen. 2:15). It was a perfect garden and God made only one condition to the man saying, "Of every tree of the garden thou mayest freely eat: But of the tree of the knowledge of good and evil, thou shalt not eat of it: for in the day that thou eatest thereof thou shalt surely die." Because of man's disobedience this garden of beauty and perfection became a garden of defeat.

In the garden of Gethsemane (John 18:1) it seemed as though the forces of the enemy were triumphant, for there Jesus was forgotten by His disciples while He prayed; He was betrayed, and He was arrested. Here was apparent defeat for the followers of Jesus and His ministry!

When the body of our Lord was laid in the tomb of the garden, there were many who believed that this spelled complete defeat for His friends (John 19:41). But the empty grave, and the blessed message—"He is Risen!"—re-echoes down through the ages to tell us—this was a real victory garden!

❦

A DIET LIST

The rivers eat away their banks,
The tides devour the sand,
The morning sun drinks up the mists,
The ocean eats the land;
Taxes eat up property,
And pride eats out the soul,—
But moths the diet record hold,
Because they eat a hole!

Remove wrappers from bars of soap and allow to dry. It will last much longer.

An economical silver polish is made by dissolving one large bar of *mild* soap in three pints of water. When this mixture is cool, but not solid, beat in one pound of whiting. The whiting only costs about 5c and this mixture will keep indefinitely in a wide mouthed jar.

Mrs. Pauline Tyley

A cloth saturated with ammonia and left in the closed oven a few hours will loosen any grease or crust caused by pies boiling over.

By serving pineapple with beans it will remove any "distress" feeling. Pineapple can be baked in with the beans or served as a salad.

Mrs. C. L. Sawyer

HOW TO REMOVE STAINS

Whenever possible remove stains when fresh to prevent them from setting. Always use cold water to remove stains made by food containing proteins, such as milk, blood, egg or meat juice. Hot water will set these stains. Use hot water for fruit and similar stains, as cold water will set them.

Blood and Meat Juice

Soak in cold or lukewarm water until stains turn light brown. Do not use hot water, as it will set the stains. Then wash in hot water, unless material is silk or wool, in which case use cold or lukewarm water. For blankets, apply a thick paste made of raw starch and cold water. Allow the paste to dry and then brush it off. Repeat until all signs of stain are gone.

Chocolate and Cocoa

If stains cannot be removed with soap and hot water, sprinkle them with borax and soak in cold water. Then rinse thoroughly in boiling water, if material is washable. For silk or wool sponge with lukewarm water.

Coffee

If stains cannot be removed by warm water and soap, pour on boiling water from a height of 2 to 3 feet. With silks, put between clean damp cloths and press with a hot iron.

Egg

Use cold water. Do not use hot water or the stains will set. Then wash with warm water and soap.

Fruit and Berry

If stains are fresh, pour on boiling water from a height of 2 to 3 feet. Repeat, if necessary, and then bleach in the sun. If this is not entirely successful, apply lemon juice to the stain and bleach in the sun.

Grass

If the stains cannot be removed by soap and warm water, apply grain or wood alcohol.

Grease

For washable materials, use warm water and soap. For silk or wool, use clean white blotting paper, a piece on each side of the stain, and iron with a warm iron. For coarse material, use cornmeal or salt, brushing off as the cornmeal or salt absorbs the grease, and repeating. Chloroform, benzol, naphtha or gasoline may also be used for sponging off grease stains, especially where dirt is mixed with grease, but these agents must be used with care.

Iodine

Make a weak solution (1 tablespoon to 1 pint of water) of baking soda, sal soda (washing soda), or borax. Wash stains in the solution and then rinse in cold water. Iodine stains are ordinarily brown, but on starchy goods are blue.

Those who say they will forgive, but can't forget an injury, simply bury the hatchet, while they leave the handle out ready for immediate use.

D. L. Moody

❧❦❧

We live charmed lives if we are living in the center of God's will. All the attacks that Satan through others can hurl against us are not only powerless to harm us, but are turned into blessings on the way.

❧❦❧

What I have done is worthy of nothing but silence and forgetfulness; but what God hath done for me is worthy of everlasting and thankful memory.

Bishop Hall

❧❦❧

A famous Chinese proverb: *"If you are planning for one year, sow grain; ten years, plant trees; but when planning for one hundred years, grow men."*

❧❦❧

Some hearts, like evening primroses, open more beautifully in the shadows of life.

❧❦❧

Temptation becomes sin when you yield to it.

❧❦❧

He who helps a child helps humanity with an immediateness which no other help given to human creature in any other stage of human life can possibly give again.

Phillips Brooks

❧❦❧

Delayed answers to prayer are not only trials of faith, but they give us opportunities of honoring God by our steadfast confidence in Him under apparent repulses.

C. H. Spurgeon

Ink

Printing ink stains may be removed by rubbing the stain thoroughly with lard, and then washing with soap and warm water. For writing inks, try washing with soap and water first. Then try cornmeal or salt or French chalk or talcum powder, brushing off as the ink is absorbed and repeating. If this is not successful soak the stains in milk for one or two days, changing the milk as it becomes discolored. Or rub the stains with a cut lemon, squeezing on some of the juice and rinsing frequently.

Iron Rust

Rub lemon juice and a little salt on the stains and bleach in the sun. Repeat or add more lemon juice if necessary.

Mildew

Moisten the stains with lemon juice, or soak overnight in sour milk, and bleach in the sun without rinsing. Or dissolve 1 pound of sal soda in 1 quart of cold water and add ¼ pound of calcium hypochloride. Apply with a medicine dropper, and IMMEDI-ATELY AFTER apply oxalic acid solution and then rinse. The immediate use of oxalic acid is to neutralize the first mixture and prevent it from harming the material. Repeat if necessary.

Milk or Cream

Use cold water. Do not use hot water, or stains will set. After using cold water, wash with soap and warm water. If material is not washable, after using cold water sponge with chloroform, gasoline or benzol.

Paint

Dip in acetone and squeeze out. Material does not need to be washed if acetone is used, and it will dry very rapidly. If acetone is not available use turpentine or benzol. Then wash with warm water and soap.

Tar, Asphalt, or Road Oil

Apply turpentine to the stains and then wash thoroughly with soap and hot water. If this is not successful, use chloroform or benzol and then wash with soap and hot water. Or try rubbing in lard and then washing with soap and hot water.

Tea

If washing with soap and warm water is not successful, apply lemon juice and bleach in the sun. Keep the stains covered with lemon juice during the bleaching.

Varnish

Rub with wood or grain alcohol or ether. Then wash with warm water and soap.

Table of Measurements

ALL measurements are level
- 1 saltspoon = ¼ teaspoon
- 3 teaspoons = 1 tablespoon
- 16 tablespoons = 1 cup
- 2 tablespoons liquid = 1 ounce
- 2 cups = 1 pint
- 4 cups = 1 quart
- 2 tablespoons sugar = 1 ounce
- 2 cups granulated sugar = 1 pound
- 2½ cups powdered sugar = 1 pound
- 2⅔ cups brown sugar = 1 pound
- 2 tablespoons butter = 1 ounce; ½ lb. = 1 cup
- 1 square chocolate = 1 ounce
- 4 cups flour = 1 pound
- 4 tablespoons flour = 1 ounce; 1 qt. = 1 lb.
- 4½ cups graham flour = 1 pound
- 1 pound suet = 4 cups chopped
- 1 large minced onion = ½ cup
- Grated rind of 1 orange = 2 tablespoons
- 1 cup raisins = 6 ounces
- 1 ounce salt = 2⅛ tablespoons

INDEX TO RECIPES

CAKES